THE GREAT BOOKS FOUNDATION

The Great Books Foundation, established in 1947, is an independent, non-profit educational organization. The sole purpose of the Foundation is to provide people of all ages with a life-long program of liberal self-education through the reading and discussion of Great Books. To implement its program of continuing education, the Foundation offers each year three hundred tuition-free courses to train volunteer discussion leaders in cities throughout the United States and Canada. In addition the Foundation helps to organize discussion groups in co-operation with interested individuals, educational institutions, public libraries, and other community agencies; prepares training and promotional material; chooses reading selections from recognized Great Books lists; and publishes inexpensive paperbound editions of Great Books readings in boxed sets for use in the program.

The Great Books Discussion Program is a unique educational activity. The program is continuous from childhood through adult life. Thousands of students participate in Junior Great Books groups, and thousands of mature men and women participate in adult groups. The program is geographically widespread, and it is possible for anyone to join a Great Books group in his own community. Finally, regardless of specialized interests, age, or extent of formal education, the program provides a common and meaningful educational experience for all those who participate.

i

Great Books discussion groups meet on a regular basis, usually once every other week. Junior groups meet in schools or libraries, adult groups in the same institutions as well as churches, business offices, and community centers—wherever adequate space and a conference table are available. Junior groups have approximately fourteen participants and, adult groups approximately twenty participants. Both Junior and adult groups are led by two volunteer co-leaders who have completed one of the Foundation's Leader Training Courses.

The Leader Training Course provides adults who wish to lead Great Books discussion groups with an understanding of how to carry out the educational objectives of the program through voluntary co-leadership. The Leader Training Course consists of eight two-hour sessions conducted by a professional staff member of the Foundation. Training courses for leaders of adult and Junior groups are held separately and a minimum enrollment of twenty-four persons is required for either type of course.

Despite limited funds, the Great Books Foundation has steadily expanded its educational program since it was founded. At present there are approximately 7,500 Great Books discussion groups in the United States and Canada. This remarkable growth has been achieved through the joint efforts of the Foundation and a large number of individual volunteers and organizations who co-sponsor Great Books Programs in their communities.

The Great Books Foundation has no financial endowment. Although its activities are supported partly by income from the sale of printed materials, the Foundation depends for its continued existence on individual gifts and bequests and on grants from philanthropic foundations.

All gifts to the Foundation are deductible for purposes of Federal Income Tax.

For further information write to the Great Books Foundation, 307 North Michigan Avenue, Chicago, Illinois 60601.

GUIDE FOR GREAT BOOKS PARTICIPANTS

The Great Books Program is based on the idea that people can help one another to learn by reading and then discussing some of the best books that have been written during the past two thousand years. The Great Books offer both a challenge and a reward. They are challenging because they force us to think about difficult and basic questions: What can we know? How should we act? What may we hope to be? These are questions that underlie everything we study, everything we do, and everything we want to make of our lives. The Great Books are rewarding because the better we understand the answers they give, the better we understand ourselves and the world around us.

In the Great Books Program there are no teachers, no tuition, no credits. The co-leaders are laymen like yourself who have taken the Foundation's Leader Training Course. Their role is to ask questions that help you to explore the ideas in the book. They are not permitted to offer answers. You may ask questions, too, but only you and your fellow participants may offer answers.

No one will tell you what answers to give. The leaders will encourage you to agree or disagree with what the author and your fellow participants say, and ask you to back up your opinions with reasons based on your reading of the book. In the process of examining and sharing ideas in the discussion, you will acquire the basis for a continuing liberal education.

The Great Books Program can help you to think clearly and independently, to express yourself effectively, and to listen attentively. To give you the best opportunity to develop these skills—and have a thoroughly good time in

*the process—you must take the responsibility for observing
the following rules:*

READ IN ADVANCE. You must complete the reading
before the meeting in order to participate in the discussion.

READ CAREFULLY. Although the meetings are not
intended to be merely an exercise in memory, you will not
get much out of the discussion unless you remember accurately what you have read. Read the entire book, or at
least portions of it, more than once. Mark passages and
make comments in the margins. Some of the things you
may wish to underline or write down are: 1) Ideas in the
book you consider important. 2) Words or passages you
do not understand. 3) Passages with which you agree or
disagree. 4) Passages about which you would like to hear
the opinions of others. 5) Passages on which you would
like to comment in the light of your own experience.
6) Passages which relate to other Great Books your group
has read and discussed.

TAKE TIME TO REFLECT. After you have read the
book carefully, pick out a few of the ideas or situations
that interest you the most. Try to increase your understanding of them by restating the ideas in your own words
or by imagining how you would act in the situations.
Finally, write down any new ideas about the book that
occur to you as a result of this exercise.

DISCUSS ONLY THE READING. Every moment of
the meeting is needed to cover even a few of the ideas in
the book. Don't introduce ideas or personal experiences,
no matter how interesting, that have nothing to do with
the book. By discussing only the book that everyone has
read, everyone will be able to follow and take part in the

discussion at all times. Don't introduce facts about the author's life and the time in which he lived unless they are mentioned in the book. Leave the names of critics and experts out of the discussion. You will learn in a Great Books discussion group only by arriving at ideas through your inquiry. No one can save you this effort. Real education is ultimately self-education.

BACK UP YOUR STATEMENTS. Don't judge a statement by who makes it or how many participants agree with it, but by how well it is supported. Statements are supported in discussion by: 1) Reading from the book. 2) Giving an accurate summary of what the book says. 3) Offering reasons or examples you think of yourself. If you repeat an opinion, definition, or idea you have heard or read elsewhere, you will be expected to back it up as if it were your own.

STICK TO THE SUBJECT UNDER DISCUSSION. You and your fellow participants should work together to explore each question fully. Try to find new ideas about what is being discussed. Don't continue to talk after you have made your point. Don't make a comment that no longer fits into the discussion; perhaps it will fit into the discussion at some later point.

DON'T TRY TO COVER THE WHOLE BOOK. You will enjoy the discussion more and understand the book better if you examine a few main ideas thoroughly. Don't jump from one idea to another in an effort to discuss all the subjects in the book.

STRIVE FOR UNDERSTANDING. Explore the meanings of the book as fully as possible, trying to resolve the issues that are raised, but realizing that not all issues can be resolved to everyone's satisfaction. A two-hour discussion serves not as an end, but only as a beginning for thinking on an issue—thinking that might come to fruition long after the discussion.

SPEAK UP FREELY. Say what you think, and be ready to give your reasons. You may agree or disagree with anything said by your fellow participants. Make your statements or ask your questions to them, not to the leaders. You need not wait to be called upon to speak.

LISTEN CAREFULLY. When others speak, do not pay so much attention to your own thoughts that you fail to hear what is said. Question them about any remark that you do not understand before you contribute your own ideas.

BE COURTEOUS. Be on time for meetings. Speak clearly so that your remarks may be heard by everyone in the room. Don't interrupt when someone else is speaking. Be willing to withhold your comments if you start to speak at the same time as others. Don't engage in private conversations. Give the leaders and your fellow participants the same respect and attention you would like for yourself.

GUIDE FOR CO-LEADERS

Every Great Books discussion group has two leaders. The purpose of the co-leaders is to conduct an exercise in reflective thinking by asking questions which will increase their own knowledge, as well as the participants', of the Great Book under discussion. To accomplish this they must: 1) ask questions that initiate, sustain, and try to conclude investigations into problems they have found in the book; 2) ask questions that challenge unclear, factually incorrect, or contradictory statements; and 3) evaluate all responses according to their best judgment —selecting those statements they want to question immediately; ignoring those they find uninteresting, trivial, or irrelevant; and tabling those they may want to pursue later. (*Manual for Co-Leaders:** Ch. I; Ch. II, "Exercise Your Options")

The value of a Great Books discussion as an educational experience depends upon how well the co-leaders carry out these three functions. Here, in summary form, are the rules and recommendations that will help you to be successful as a co-leader. The *Manual* provides you with a complete explanation of the method of discussion. The Leader Training Course will give you the opportunity to see it demonstrated and to apply it yourself. (Ch. III)

* The references are to *A Manual for Co-Leaders,* which may be obtained from the Great Books Foundation for $1.75 a copy. Also available from the Foundation are Reader Aids (suggested questions for discussion) at $1.00 for each set, and *The Gadfly,* a bimonthly publication of the Liberal Arts, free to contributors of $3.00 or more a year to the Great Books Foundation.

RECOGNIZE THE THREE KINDS OF QUESTIONS YOU CAN ASK ABOUT THE BOOK. These are questions of fact, questions of interpretation, and questions of evaluation. 1) The "facts" of a Great Book are the author's words, everything he has written down in the selection. Questions of fact require the participant to offer quotations from, or paraphrases of the book. 2) Questions of interpretation ask the participant to explore what the author means by what he has said. 3) Questions of evaluation ask the participant to determine in what respects he agrees or disagrees with the author's meaning, or to what extent the book has application to his own life. (Ch. II, "Recognizing the Differences Among Questions of Fact, Interpretation, and Evaluation")

STRESS QUESTIONS OF INTERPRETATION, BUT KNOW WHEN TO USE QUESTIONS OF FACT AND EVALUATION. Because your purpose is to increase your own and the participants' understanding of the book, favor questions of interpretation. However, if the group is not accurately remembering what the author said, or is offering interpretations which are factually incorrect, doubtful, or insufficiently documented, ask questions of fact. But don't allow the discussion to become merely an exercise in memory.

Questions of evaluation are meaningful only after the group has thoroughly discussed related questions of interpretation. Questions of evaluation may look like an easy way to get a discussion started, but they can quickly turn the discussion into a polling of likes and dislikes, or a defense of premature or hasty judgments. Questions of evaluation should always concern themselves with the truth or application of ideas from the book. They should not be allowed to lead to a discussion of subjects that do not require the use of the book; otherwise the discussion loses its purpose and becomes a recital of opinions about abstract terms and topical events. (Ch. II, "Stress Questions of Interpretation, but Know When to Ask Questions of Fact and Evaluation")

FORMULATE BASIC QUESTIONS THAT ARE INTERPRETIVE. Basic questions are always interpretative questions that can lead to an extended discussion of what you and your co-leader consider some of the main ideas or actions in the book. They are questions through which you hope to increase your knowledge of the book because either you do not have a satisfactory answer to them or you do not believe your answers are the only acceptable ones. Basic questions are likely to generate opposing or different responses which will help to clarify and develop the ideas you believe are important. Ask basic questions that you care about and that reflect your deepest level of insight. Don't ask a question to which you are looking for a particular answer as a springboard to a basic question. Ask the basic question instead. (Ch. II, "Basic Questions Are Interpretive"; "Formulating Basic Questions You Care About")

KNOW WHEN TO ASK BASIC QUESTIONS. A basic question should be used: 1) To begin the discussion. 2) When the participants introduce a problem which greatly interests them and which you and your co-leader are prepared to develop. 3) When the subject under discussion is apparently exhausted. (Ch. II, "When to Ask Basic Questions")

KNOW WHEN TO ASK FOLLOW-UP QUESTIONS. From the standpoint of the movement of discussion, all

questions which are not basic are classified as follow-up
questions. They contain ideas that are subordinate but related to the basic question. Follow-up questions examine
the responses of participants; their main function is to help
the group to resolve the basic question. (Ch. II, "Recognizing the Differences Among Questions of Fact, Interpretation, and Evaluation")

Follow-up questions are asked either by you or the
participants, with these purposes in mind: 1) To introduce
some of the implications of the basic question. 2) To
require a participant to substantiate a statement or opinion
with a quotation from, or a paraphrase of the book. 3) To
elicit more opinions about the subject being dscussed.
4) To clarify a statement. 5) To develop what you think is
the most important idea in a participant's response. 6) To
encourage the participant to examine his remarks in terms
of their consequences and consistency. 7) To bring the
discussion back to the book. (Ch. II, "When to Ask Follow-
Up Questions")

DEVELOP A DISCUSSION IN DEPTH. Stick with the
subject introduced by your basic question in order to
develop all of its implications. Give the group time to think
of the book in terms of your basic question. You may have
to ask the same question of several participants or rephrase
it without changing the subject. (Ch. II, "Develop a Discussion in Depth")

STRIVE FOR ANSWERS. Don't be content with superficial responses or attempts by the participants to leave a
question just because it is difficult. Use their answers as the
basis for new questions that will help the group to reach a
deeper understanding of the book. At the same time, keep
in mind that some questions asked in a Great Books

discussion cannot be answered to everyone's satisfaction. (Ch. II, "Strive for Answers")

DO NOT INTRODUCE DIFFICULT OR TECHNICAL TERMS. If you introduce terms that are difficult to define, such as free will, satire, and tragedy, when they are not in the book, you interrupt the group's exploration of the author's meaning by diverting their attention to words that cannot be defined in context. You encourage the group to use impressive sounding words as a substitute for thinking about the book in more specific language. You also deprive the group of those moments of discovery when they find their own words to embody the ideas they have been examining. Terms that arise in this manner can be the high point of the meeting and provide an excellent means for you and the participants to remember the discussion. (Ch. II, "Try Not to Introduce Difficult or Technical Terms")

WORD YOUR QUESTIONS CAREFULLY. Ask one question at a time and keep your questions brief and clear. Long, involved questions indicate that you haven't given enough thought to an idea. Try to ask questions tailored to the book under discussion rather than general questions which would apply with little or no change to any number of books. Avoid questions that indicate the answers you expect, questions that cannot be answered from a reading of the book, or questions that force the participant to draw on outside material. (Ch. II, "Word Your Questions Carefully")

LISTEN INTENTLY. This will help you to ask relevant follow-up questions. It will also give you ideas for basic questions and indicate whether a particular line of inquiry should be abandoned. (Ch. II, "Listen Intently")

INVOLVE EACH PARTICIPANT. Invite participants into the discussion by prefacing your question with the name of the person to whom you want to direct it. Make sure questions are directed to every participant during each meeting. Encourage participants to ask each other questions and to speak up freely without raising their hands or waiting to be acknowledged by the leaders. Seat everyone around a table or in a circle; the physical arrangement reinforces the idea of equal participation. (Ch. II, "Involve Each Participant")

OBSERVE THE BASIC RULES OF DISCUSSION. They help the participants to think for themselves and to insure maximum use of the time for discussion of the books.

Rule 1. The group may discuss only the book assigned for the meeting or books discussed at previous meetings.

Rule 2. No participant may take part in the discussion who has not read the book.

Rule 3. Participants may not introduce outside authorities to lend weight to their opinions.

Rule 4. As a co-leader you may only ask questions. You may never introduce your opinions or make comments, even when you believe that participants are making an error of fact or judgment.

Rule 5. There must be two co-leaders for each discussion. (Ch. II, "Observe the Basic Rules of Discussion")

READ CAREFULLY. The questions you decide to ask your group evolve from a thorough and thoughtful reading of the book. Write down questions as they occur to you. Questions originate in the following sources: 1) Ideas in the book you consider interesting or important. 2) Words or passages that you don't understand. 3) Passages that have multiple meanings and implications. 4) Attempts to connect ideas in the book. 5) Passages whose truthfulness or application you would like the participants to consider in the light of their own experience. (Ch. III, "Read Carefully")

DISCUSS THE BOOK IN ADVANCE WITH YOUR CO-LEADER. Alternating as participant and co-leader, try to answer both your sets of questions. Sharpen the questions you believe will prompt an interesting and profitable examination of the book. Drop questions that do not seem to go anywhere. Write down new questions that arise from your discussion. Arrange all questions in clusters, distinguishing those that are basic from those that may be appropriate as follow-up questions. Agree with your co-leader about the basic questions you wish to ask the group. (Ch. III, "Pre-Discussion")

MEET WITH YOUR CO-LEADER AFTER THE DISCUSSION. Between yourselves attempt to answer two important questions: 1) Have you learned anything new about the book? 2) What could you have done to improve the discussion? The key to growth as a leader is learning something new about the book and your technique of discussion as a result of each Great Books meeting. (Ch. III, "Evaluation: Post Discussion")

Ten Dont's for Co-Leaders

1) Don't ask questions to which you are sure you know the answers, and then try to steer the group to arrive at your insights or conclusions.

2) Don't slip your opinions into the discussion in the

guise of questions. (*Don't you think Creon showed more pride than Antigone? Do you think* right *in* The Declaration of Independence *means* just claim *because if it means* duty *you would have a redundancy at one point in the document, and if it means* gift, *then you are implying that the colonists would change their government because a gift was taken away from them?*)

3) Don't emphasize questions exploring the participants' personal experiences or preferences as opposed to questions dealing with the author's intention or meaning. (*Did you like the book? What did you learn from it? Do you think the selection is a Great Book? Do you agree with the author? Will the book enrich your life?*)

4) Don't ask general questions that could, with little change in wording, be asked about many other books. (*What is the book about? What kind of person is*_____ [any character in the book]? *What conclusion did the author come to about* _____ [any idea or topic in the book]?) By asking such questions you put little reflective thought into the discussion and therefore should not expect to draw much out.

5) Don't keep switching the subject under discussion.

6) Don't assume you can develop a discussion in depth without following up continuously on your basic question.

7) Don't ignore the responses of participants when you formulate follow-up questions during discussion.

8) Don't use technical or difficult terms that cannot readily be defined from a reading of the book. (*Is* Macbeth *a tragedy? Is* Gulliver's Travels *a satire? Is the Prologue-Epilogue technique of* The Canterbury Tales *a literary appendage?*)

9) Don't ask questions that do not indicate immediately the problem you wish to explore. (*Did Antigone commit a*

crime?) From this wording of this question the participants cannot tell whether you are asking for Creon's opinion, Sophocles', or their own.

10) Don't ask several questions at the same time. (*Why does Antigone bury Polyneices twice, and why doesn't Ismene help her?*)

CHRONOLOGICAL LIST OF THE AUTHORS YOU WILL READ IN THE FIRST 5 SETS OF THE ADULT GREAT BOOKS SERIES

Homer	*c.*900 B.C.
Aeschylus	525–456 B.C.
Sophocles	*c.*496–*c.*406 B.C.
Euripides	*c.*484–*c.*406 B.C.
Thucydides	*c.*460–*c.*400 B.C.
Aristophanes	*c.*448–*c.*380 B.C.
Plato	*c.*427–*c.*347 B.C.
Aristotle	384–322 B.C.
Vergil	70–19 B.C.
St. Matthew	?
St. Paul	?–*c.*A.D. 67
Plutarch	*c.*A.D. 46–*c.*120
Epictetus	*c.*A.D. 60–*c.*118
St. Augustine	*c.*353–*c.*430
St. Thomas Aquinas	1225–1274
Dante Alighieri	1265–1321
Giovanni Boccaccio	1313–1375
Geoffrey Chaucer	1340–1400
Niccolo Machiavelli	1469–1527
Michel de Montaigne	1533–1592
William Shakespeare	1564–1616
Thomas Hobbes	1588–1679
René Descartes	1596–1650

Karl Marx	1818–1883
Ivan Turgenev	1818–1883
Herman Melville	1819–1891
Friedrich Engels	1820–1895
Fyodor Dostoyevsky	1821–1881
Henrik Ibsen	1828–1906
Leo Tolstoy	1828–1910
Henry Adams	1838–1918
William James	1842–1910
Henry James	1843–1916
Friedrich Nietzsche	1844–1900
Henri Poincaré	1854–1912
Sigmund Freud	1856–1939
George Bernard Shaw	1856–1950
Joseph Conrad	1857–1924
Thorstein Veblen	1857–1929
Henri Bergson	1859–1941
Anton Chekhov	1860–1904
Thomas Mann	1875–1955
James Joyce	1882–1941

SELECTIONS FROM THE FIRST FIVE SETS OF THE ADULT SERIES CLASSIFIED ACCORDING TO SUBJECT MATTER

PHILOSOPHY	THEOLOGY	HISTORY AND SOCIAL SCIENCE	SCIENCE AND METHOD	DRAMA	OTHER LITERATURE
Apology; Crito (1)*	The Book of Genesis (4)	The Peloponnesian War (3)	Discourse on Method (2)	Oresteia (3)	The Odyssey (2)
The Republic (4)	The Book of Job (3)	Politics (3)	The First Dialogue between Hylas and Philonous (4)	Antigone (1)	The Aeneid (4)
Symposium (5)	Euthyphro (2)	Pompey (1)		Oedipus Rex; Oedipus at Colonus (2)	The Inferno (5)
Ethics (2)	The Gospel According To St. Matthew (1)	The Ruler (1)	The Origin of Species (5)	Medea; Hippolytus (5)	The Decameron (5)
Poetics (3)	Corinthians I; Romans (5)	Of Civil Government (1)	An Introduction to the Study of Experimental Medicine (4)	Peace; The Birds (3)	The Canterbury Tales (5)
The Manual of Epictetus (5)	The Confessions of St. Augustine (3)	The Social Contract (3)		Hamlet (2)	Gulliver's Travels (2)
Essays of Montaigne (4)	Summa Theologica: Treatise on Law (3)	The Wealth of Nations (1)	Psychology: Briefer Course (5)	King Lear (3)	Candide (3)
Leviathan (2)	Pensées (2)	The Declaration of Independence (1)	The Value of Science (2)	Macbeth (1)	Rameau's Nephew (4)
On the Improvement of the Understanding (5)	Works of Love (5)	Perpetual Peace (1)	A General Introduction to Psychoanalysis (2)	Life is a Dream (4)	The Overcoat (2)
An Enquiry Concerning Human Understanding (4)		The Federalist Papers (1)		The Misanthrope; Tartuffe (4)	Walden (1)
Foundations of the Metaphysics of Morals (5)		The Decline and Fall of the Roman Empire (3)		Phaedra (4)	Fathers and Sons (5) Billy Budd, Foretopman (2)
Twilight of the Idols (3)		Democracy in America (1)		Faust (5)	Notes from Underground (4)
Civilization and Its Discontents (3)		The Autobiography of John Stuart Mill (4)		The Wild Duck (5)	The Death of Ivan Ilych (1)
Time and Free Will (5)		On Liberty (2)		Heartbreak House (3)	The Pupil; The Beast in the Jungle (4)
		Civil Disobediance (1)		The Three Sisters; The Cherry Orchard (4)	Heart of Darkness (4)
		The Communist Manifesto (1)			Death in Venice (3)
		The Education of Henry Adams (4)			Dubliners (1)
		The Theory of the Leisure Class (4)			

* Number in parentheses shows Adult Set in which work will be found.

THE GREAT BOOKS FOUNDATION

SET TWO
VOLUME TWO

4
ARISTOTLE
Ethics

5
ST. AUGUSTINE
Confessions of St. Augustine

THE GREAT BOOKS ADULT SERIES: SET TWO

ARISTOTLE

Ethics

Books I and VII

NUMBER 4 | SET TWO

THE GREAT BOOKS FOUNDATION Chicago

published and distributed by
THE GREAT BOOKS FOUNDATION
a non-profit educational organization
307 North Michigan Avenue, Chicago, Illinois 60601

CONTENTS

I. THE END OF HUMAN LIFE

Contents

VII. THE IDEAL LIFE

I The End of Human Life

A. PREFATORY: SUBJECT OF THE PRESENT INQUIRY

1. THE GOAL OF HUMAN ACTIVITY

EVERY art and every inquiry, and likewise every action and pursuit, is believed to aim at some good. The good has therefore been rightly declared to be 'that at which all things aim.' But ends differ to some extent among themselves: some are activities, others are products distinct from these; and in the latter case the products are naturally more worth having than the activities. Now since there is a great variety of actions, arts and sciences, there are correspondingly numerous ends: health is the end of medical science, a vessel that of shipbuilding, victory that of strategy, wealth that of economics. Wherever such arts, etc., can be classified as members of a single skill,[1] the ends of the master arts are preferable to all the subordinate ends; for it is with a view to the former that the latter are pursued. It makes no difference whether the activities are ends in themselves, or something else distinct from them (as in the case of the sciences mentioned in the foregoing note).

2. HUMAN GOOD THE OBJECT OF SOCIAL SCIENCE

If then there is some end of the things we do, an end which we desire for its own sake and for which all else

[1] Bridle-making, for instance, and the other arts dealing with the equipment of horses fall under the art of equitation, and this latter and every military action under strategy, and so on with other branches of art.

1

is desired—that is to say, if we do not do everything for the sake of something else[1]—obviously this end will be the Good, i.e. the best of all things. Knowledge of it must accordingly exercise a profound influence upon life; if, like archers, we have a target, we shall be more likely to hit upon what is right. We must therefore attempt to determine, at any rate in outline, what that knowledge is, i.e. to which of the arts or practical sciences it belongs. This will be recognized as the most authoritative, i.e. as that which is most truly the master art or science. Now social science appears to be of this nature; it lays down which of the sciences are to be taught in city-states, and which of them each class of citizens is to learn, and up to what point. We also find that even the most honourable of skills, e.g. strategy, economics, rhetoric, come within the province of social science. Since the latter makes use of all other practical sciences, and since again it lays down the law as to what we must do and from what abstain, the end of social science must include those of the others, and must accordingly be man's good. For although the end is the same for an individual and for a city-state, that of the state seems at any rate a greater and more complete thing whether to retain or to preserve; to secure the good of one man is better than nothing, but it is more noble and godlike to do so for a whole people or for city-states. These therefore are the ends to which our inquiry is directed.

[1] If we did, the process would go on *ad infinitum,* so that our desire would be ineffectual and vain.

OUR discussion will be adequate if it has as much clarity as the subject-matter allows; absolute precision must not be sought alike in all discussions any more than in all products of the various crafts. Now fine and just actions, which are the province of social science, give rise to so much variety and fluctuation in men's judgments that they are believed to exist by convention alone, and not by nature. The recognized good things of life also give rise to such fluctuation, because many people suffer harm on their account; it is no new thing for men to come to grief through wealth, or as a result of their courage. It is therefore sufficient when speaking on such a subject and with such premises to indicate the truth roughly and in outline, and when speaking about things which are no more than approximately true and with like premises to arrive at conclusions of the same character. Each sort of statement should be received in the same way, for it is the part of an educated man to expect precision in any branch of science only in so far as the nature of the subject allows; it is surely just as absurd to admit probable reasoning from a mathematician as to ask a rhetorician for scientific demonstration.

Now each man judges aright of the things he knows, and of these he is a good judge. He, therefore, who has been trained in any particular subject is a good judge of it, and he who has received a comprehensive education is a good all-round judge. Consequently a young man is unsuited to attend lectures on social science; he has no experience of life's activities, from which its discussions arise and with which they deal. Moreover, since he is

inclined to follow his passions, he will study in vain and without the least profit, because the end is not knowledge but action. Nor does it make any difference whether he is young in age or in character; his deficiency is due not to lack of years but to the fact that he lives and pursues every object in obedience to passion. With such people, as with the morally weak, knowledge serves no useful purpose; but to those who desire and act consistently knowledge of such matters will be most beneficial.

C. WHAT IS THE GOOD FOR MAN?

1. THE GOOD FOR MAN COMMONLY SAID TO BE HAPPINESS

DISPUTE AS TO THE NATURE OF HAPPINESS

RESUMING now, and having regard to the fact that all knowledge and every pursuit is directed to the attainment of some good, let us state our view as to the end of social science, i.e. as to the highest of all goods that can be achieved by action. As regards its name there is almost complete agreement; both the ordinary run of men and persons of superior refinement say that it is happiness, i.e. they suppose that living well and doing well are the same as being happy. But as regards the exact nature of happiness there is a difference of opinion; the common herd does not give the same account of it as do the wise. The former hold it to be some plain and obvious thing like pleasure, riches or honour; but they differ among themselves,[1] and being aware of their ignorance they admire those who propound some grand theory which is above their comprehension. Some of these latter used to think that over and above the many good things we know there is another good which is self-subsistent and the cause of the goodness of all the good things we know. It would, I think, be rather a waste of time to study every one of the opinions that have been held; enough to examine those that are most prevalent or that seem plausible.

[1] It often happens indeed that one and the same man identifies happiness with different things—with health when he is sick, with wealth when he is poor.

Let us not, however, overlook the fact that there is a difference between arguments *a priori* and *a posteriori*. Plato used rightly to pose this question: 'Are we on the way *from* or *to* the first principles?' There is a difference, as there is on a race-track between the course from the judges to the turning post and the return road. For while we have to start from what is known, things are objects of knowledge in two senses: some to us, others without qualification. It would seem, therefore, that *we* must make a start from things known to *us*. Consequently a man who is to listen with profit to lectures on what is noble and just and, in general, on the subjects covered by social science, must have been brought up to good habits. For the definition of happiness (whatever we discover it to be) is the starting-point or first principle, and if this is sufficiently clear to him he will not at the outset require any knowledge of metaphysics or of physics; and the man who has been properly brought up has or can easily get starting points. Anyone who neither has nor can get them should bear in mind the words of Hesiod:

> He is far best who knows all things himself;
> Good, the man who listens to sage counsel;
> But one who neither knows, nor takes to heart
> Another's wisdom, is a useless dolt.

2. POPULAR VIEWS OF THE GOOD

Let us, however, go back to the point at which we digressed. Most men, i.e. men of the most vulgar sort, appear (as might be expected from the lives they lead) to identify the good, or happiness, with pleasure; and this is just why they love the life of enjoyment. But there are three outstanding types of life: (*a*) the one just mentioned, (*b*) the political and (*c*) the contempla-

tive. Now as regards (*a*), the majority of people are manifestly altogether slavish in their tastes, preferring a life
similar to that of beasts; they obtain a hearing because
many of those in high positions share the tastes of Sardan-
apalus. As regards (*b*), consideration of the principal
types of life shows that persons of superior refinement and
active disposition identify happiness with honour; for this
is, roughly speaking, the goal of political life. It is, however, clearly too superficial to be what we are seeking; for
it is regarded as dependent on those who confer honour
rather than on the person honoured, whereas we divine the
good to be something proper to a man and of which he is
not easily deprived. Again, men seem to pursue honour in
order to persuade themselves that they are good; at least
they seek to be honoured by men of practical wisdom,
among those who know them, and on account of their
virtue. Evidently then, in their view at any rate, virtue is
better. Indeed one might perhaps suppose virtue, rather
than honour, to be the end of political life. But even this
appears somewhat incomplete; for it seems possible for
a man to possess virtue and yet to be asleep or to pass
his whole life in a state of inactivity, and, furthermore, to
endure the greatest sufferings and misfortunes; but no
one, unless he were defending a thesis to the last ditch,
would describe a man who lived thus as happy. But
enough of this; sufficient has been said on the subject in
discussions and writings outside this school. Finally (*c*)
we have the contemplative life, with which we shall deal
later on. As for the money-maker, he is under compulsion,
and wealth is clearly not the good we are seeking; for it
is merely useful and has something else in view. Therefore one might rather take pleasure, honour and virtue
as ends, for they are cherished for their own sakes. But

it is plain that not even these are ends, so plain in fact that the many diatribes against them are hardly necessary. Anyway, let us leave this subject.

3. THE PLATONIC IDEA OF GOOD

We must next consider the universal Good and go carefully into the question of what is meant by it, although such an inquiry is rendered an uphill affair by the fact that the Forms have been imported by my own friends. Yet we must surely admit that it is better, and indeed our duty, for the sake of upholding truth even to destroy what touches us closely, especially as we are philosophers; for while both are dear, truth has the first call upon our respect.

Those who introduced this doctrine did not invent Ideas of classes within which they recognized priority and posterity.[1] Now the term 'good' is used in the category of substance, in that of quality and in that of relation, and the essential, i.e. substance, is prior in nature to the relative (which is like an offshoot and accident of substance); so there could not be a common Idea covering all these goods.

Again, since 'good' is used in as many senses as the word 'is,'[2] clearly it cannot be something universally present in all cases and single; if it were it could not have been predicated in all the categories, but in one only.

Moreover, since things corresponding to one Idea are the objects of one science, there would have to be one

[1] This is why they did not devise an Idea of number.

[2] It is predicated in the category of substance, as of God and of reason; in that of quality, as of the virtues; in that of quantity, as of the moderate; in that of relation, as of the useful; in that of time, as of the right opportunity; in that of place, as of the right locality and the like.

Idea of all goods. In fact, however, there are many sciences even of the things that fall under one category, e.g. of opportunity; for opportunity in war is studied by strategy and in disease by therapy, just as moderation in food is studied by medicine and in exercise by gymnastics.

One might also raise the question as to what on earth they can mean by 'a thing in itself,' seeing that the account of man is one and the same in the case of (*a*) 'man as such' and (*b*) a particular man. For in so far as both (*a*) and (*b*) are man they will differ in no respect whatever; and if this is so, nor will 'good itself' and particular goods differ in so far as they are good. Furthermore, 'good itself' will not be good any the more for being eternal, since that which endures for long is no whiter than that which lasts only for a day. The Pythagoreans seem to offer a more convincing account of the good, placing unity in the category of goods; and Speusippus seems to have followed them. But let us discuss these matters elsewhere.

What we have been saying may be called in question on the grounds that Plato's words do not apply to *every* good, and that the goods pursued and loved for themselves are called good by reference to a single Form, whereas those which tend to produce these or to preserve them in some way or to prevent their contraries are called so in a different sense, i.e. because of their effects. Obviously, therefore, goods must be spoken of in two ways: some must be good in themselves, and others on account of these. So let us separate things good in themselves from useful things, and inquire whether the former are called good by reference to a single Idea. What kind of goods would one describe as good in themselves?

Shall we say those that are pursued even in isolation from others, e.g. intelligence, sight and certain pleasures and honours? It is certain that even if we pursue these for the sake of something else, one would still rank them among things good in themselves. Or are we to say that nothing is good in itself except the Idea of good? If so the Form will be purposeless. On the other hand, if intelligence, sight, etc., are also things good in themselves, the definition of the good will have to appear the same in them all, as that of whiteness is the same in snow as in white lead. But the definitions of honour, wisdom and pleasure, *in so far as these latter are good,* are distinct and different from one another. Consequently the good is not some common element answering to one Idea.

In what sense then are all goods so called? Surely not in the sense of things which have a mere accidental identity of name. Is it perhaps by virtue of their being derived from a single good or by all conducing to one good? Or are they rather one by analogy? Certainly as sight is in the body, so is reason in the soul, and so forth. But perhaps we had better leave these matters for the time being; complete accuracy about them would be more appropriate to another branch of philosophy. And similarly as regards the Idea; even if there is some one good universally predicated of goods or having separate and independent existence, clearly it must be beyond man's achievement or attainment, whereas we are at present looking for something that *is* attainable. Perhaps, however, someone might think it worth while to recognize this unattainable with a view to such goods as *can* be attained and achieved; he may urge that, having it as a sort of pattern, we shall know better the goods that are good for us, and if we know them we shall lay hold on them.

Well, there is some degree of cogency in this argument, but it seems to be at variance with the sciences; for all of these, while aiming at some good and seeking to supply the lack of it, do not concern themselves with knowledge of *the* good. Yet it is unlikely that all practitioners of the arts should be ignorant of and should not even look for so great an aid. It is difficult, moreover, to see how a weaver or a carpenter will be assisted in regard to his particular craft by knowing this 'good in itself,' or how the man who has beheld the Idea itself will be a better doctor or a better general on that account. For the doctor appears not even to study health in this way, but the health of man—or rather, surely, that of a particular man, since the healing art is applied to individuals. Enough, however, of this question.

4. THE GOOD FINAL AND SELF-SUFFICIENT. HOW THE DEFINITION OF HAPPINESS IS REACHED

Let us make a fresh start in our search for man's good. It seems to vary from one action and art to another; for it is one thing in medicine, another in strategy, and so on in the rest of the arts. What then is the good of each? Surely that for the sake of which all else is done. In medicine this is health, in strategy victory, in architecture a house, and so forth—the end, in fact, of any given action or pursuit; for it is with a view to this that all men do whatever else they do. Consequently, if there be an end (or ends) of all that we do, this (or these) must be the good (or goods) attainable by action.

So the argument has by shifting its ground reached the same point; but we must endeavour to state this with even greater clarity. Since there are manifestly more ends than one, and we choose some of these (e.g. wealth, flutes and instruments in general) for the sake of something else, it is clear that not all ends are final. But the supreme good is evidently something final; hence, if there is only one final end, this will be what we are looking for. Now we call that which is in itself worthy of pursuit more final than that which is worthy of pursuit for the sake of something else, and that which is never desirable for the sake of something else more final than things which are desirable both in themselves and for the sake of that other thing; and therefore it is without qualification that we apply the epithet 'final' to that which is always desirable in itself and never for the sake of something else.

Now happiness more than anything else is looked upon as some such thing, for we choose it always for its own sake and never for that of something else. Honour, pleasure, reason and every virtue we choose indeed for themselves,[1] but we choose them also for the sake of happiness, supposing that by their means we shall be happy. No one, on the other hand, chooses happiness for the sake of these, nor for anything at all except itself.

The same conclusion seems to be reached from the standpoint of self-sufficiency, for the final good is held to be self-sufficient. Now since man is by nature a social being we do not mean by 'self-sufficient' that which suffices for a man by himself, one who leads an isolated life, but that which suffices also for his parents, children, wife and indeed for his friends and fellow citizens. Some limit, of course, must be set to the notions expressed by 'parents,' 'children' and 'friends'; for if they are extended to include ancestors, descendants and friends' friends,

---

[1] For if nothing came of them we would still choose them one and all.

we are heading for an infinite series. Let us, however, defer the study of this question. We now define the self-sufficient as that which all on its own makes life desirable and lacking in nothing. Such we think happiness to be; further, we think it not just one good thing among others,[1] but the most desirable thing of all. Happiness then is something final and self-sufficient, and is the goal of activity.

But surely to identify happiness and the chief good seems platitudinous; we still need a clearer account of what happiness is. This might perhaps be forthcoming if we could first ascertain the function of man. For just as in the case of a flautist, a sculptor or any artist, and generally in the case of anything whatever that has a function or activity, the good and the 'well' are considered to reside in that function, so also it would seem to be in the case of man, if he has a function. Are we going to say that the carpenter and the tanner have certain functions or activities, but that man as such has none—that he is born without a function? Surely it is reasonable to suppose that man has a function distinct from those of the eye, hand and foot, each of which undoubtedly has one. The question is what in the world can that function be? Life seems to be common even to vegetables, but we are looking for what is peculiar to *man*. We must therefore exclude the life of growth and reproduction. Next, there is sentient life, but this also appears to be common even to the horse, the ox and every animal. There remains then an active life of the rational element. But since 'life of

---

[1] If it were thus included among other good things it would clearly be rendered more desirable still by the addition of the least of goods; for what is added becomes an excess of goods, and of goods the greater is always more desirable.

the rational element' also has a twofold meaning, we must state that we are referring to life in the sense of activity; and indeed this seems to be the more proper sense of the term. Now if the function of man is an activity of soul which follows or implies a rational principle, and if we say 'a so-and-so' and 'a good so-and-so' have a function which is generically the same,[1] then the good for man turns out to be activity of soul in accordance with virtue, or, if there is more than one virtue, in accordance with the best and most complete. But it is necessary to add 'in a complete life.' For one swallow does not make a summer, nor does a single day; and likewise one day or a brief period does not make man blessed and happy.

So much for an outline of the good; it is right, I think, to make a rough sketch first and fill in the details later. It would seem, however, that anyone is capable of developing and articulating what has been well outlined, and that time is a good discoverer or collaborator in such a task; hence the advances made in the arts, for what is lacking may be supplied by anyone. We must also recall what has already been said about not expecting absolute precision in all things, but only such precision as the subject-matter in each case allows and to such an extent as is appropriate to the inquiry. A carpenter and a geometer study the right angle in different ways: the former investigates it in so far as it is useful to his craft; the latter seeks to know what it is or what sort of thing it is, for he is a spectator of the truth. The same course, then,

---

[1] e.g. a harpist and a good harpist, and so without qualification in all cases, the excess in goodness (of the good individual over the individual simply) being added to the function, for the function of a harpist is to play the harp, and that of a good harpist to do so well.

must be followed in all other matters as well, lest side issues end by taking precedence of the main task. Nor must the *cause* be demanded in all cases alike; it is sometimes enough that the *fact* be clearly demonstrated, as in the case of first principles; the fact is the primary thing or first principle. Now we apprehend some first principles by induction, others by intuition, others by some form of habituation, and others again in other ways. But we must try to investigate each set of principles in accordance with their nature, and we must take care that they are stated correctly, since they have a great influence upon what follows. For the beginning is thought to be more than half of the whole, and to provide answers to many of the questions raised.

5. DEFINITION OF HAPPINESS SUPPORTED BY COMMON BELIEFS

We must now examine our definition of the Good for Man not only in the light of our conclusion and premises, but also in that of common opinion; for current moral judgments all harmonize with a true view, but established facts soon clash with a false one. Now goods have been divided into three groups: some are described as external, others as relating to soul, others again as relating to body. Men call those that relate to soul most properly and truly goods, and they classify psychical actions and activities as relating to soul. Our definition, therefore, will be right, at any rate according to this opinion, which is of long standing and generally accepted by philosophers. It is likewise correct inasmuch as the end is identified with certain actions and activities, whereby it comes to rank among goods of the soul and not among external goods. Also in harmony with our account is the belief that the

happy man lives well and does well; for we have practically defined happiness as a kind of good life and good
activity. Again, all the features looked for in happiness
appear to belong to what we have defined happiness as
being. For some regard it as identical with virtue, others
with practical wisdom, others with a kind of speculative
wisdom, others with these or one of them, together with
pleasure or not without pleasure; and others again include external prosperity. Now some of these opinions
have been widely held by ancient thinkers, others by a
few eminent men. It is not likely that either of these
groups should be wholly in error; it is more probable that
they should be right in at least some one respect or even
in most respects.

Our definition harmonizes with the view of those who
maintain that happiness is virtue, or some particular virtue; for virtuous activity is part of virtue. It may, however, make no small difference whether we place the
chief good in possession or in use, in state of mind or in
activity. For it is possible for the state of mind to exist
and yet produce no good result;[1] not so with the activity,
because one who has it will necessarily be acting, and
acting well. Just as in the Olympic Games it is not the
most beautiful or the strongest that are crowned, but those
who compete (because from these latter the victors are
drawn), so also those who act are the rightful winners of
the noble and good things in life. Their life also is pleasant
in itself; for pleasure is among the states of soul, and to
every man that of which he is said to be a lover is
pleasant. Thus a horse is pleasant to the lover of horses,
a spectacle to the lover of shows; and in the same way
just acts are pleasant to the lover of justice and virtuous

[1] e.g. in a man who is asleep or otherwise inactive.

acts in general to the lover of virtue. Now in the case of most men their pleasures are in mutual conflict, because those pleasures are not by nature pleasant; but men who love what is noble find pleasant those things which are by nature pleasant. But virtuous actions are by nature pleasant, and are therefore pleasant not only in themselves but also to lovers of what is noble. Consequently the life of such people has no additional need of pleasure as a kind of superfluous ornament, but finds its pleasure within itself. For, besides what we have already said, he who does not rejoice in noble actions is not even good. After all, no one would call a man just who did not enjoy acting justly, nor any man liberal who did not enjoy liberal actions, and so on. Virtuous actions, therefore, must be in themselves pleasant. But they are also good and noble, and possess each of these attributes in the highest degree; for the good man judges well about these attributes, and his judgment is as we have described. Happiness then is the best, the noblest and the most pleasant thing on earth, and these attributes are not separated one from another as in the inscription at Delos:

> Noblest is that which is most just, and best is health;
> But pleasantest it is to obtain what one loves.

For *all* these properties belong to the best activities; and with these, or with one (the best) of these, we identify happiness.

Nevertheless, as we remarked earlier on, happiness obviously needs the external goods as well; for it is difficult, if not impossible, to perform noble acts without the necessary equipment. In many actions we employ friends and wealth and political power as instruments. There are also some things whose absence takes the gilt off happiness, e.g. good birth, good children, beauty; for the man who is very ugly in appearance or low-born or solitary and childless is not likely to be happy, and still less likely perhaps if he has rascally children or friends, or has been robbed by death of good children or friends. As we said, therefore, happiness seems to require this kind of prosperity also; for which reason some equate happiness with good fortune, though others identify it with virtue.

6. HOW IS HAPPINESS ACQUIRED?

It is just this fact which gives rise to the difficulty as to whether happiness is to be acquired by learning or by habituation or by some other discipline, or occurs as the fruit of some divine dispensation, or again by chance. Well, if there is *any* such thing as a gift of the gods to men, it is reasonable that happiness should be god-given, and most assuredly so among all human things inasmuch as it is the best. This question would perhaps be more appropriate to another branch of study. Yet happiness, even if it is not heaven-sent but arises from virtue via some form of learning or training, seems to be among the most godlike things; for that which is the prize and end of virtue is obviously the best thing—something godlike and blessed. Nevertheless, it must be very widely shared; for it is accessible, through a certain kind of study and care, to all whose capacity for virtue has not been maimed. Now if it is better to be happy thus than by chance, it is reasonable that the facts should be as suggested, since everything dependent on nature is by nature as good as it can be, and similarly all that depends on art or any rational cause, especially if it depends on the best of all causes. To entrust what is greatest and most noble to chance would be a highly unsatisfactory arrangement.

The answer to our question is plain also from the definition of happiness. We have said that this is activity of a certain kind, and that some external goods must necessarily be present as preconditions of happiness, while others are by nature co-operative and useful as instruments. And this of course is in agreement with what we said at the outset, viz. that the end of social science is the best end, because social science devotes itself chiefly to making citizens of a certain quality, i.e. good and capable of noble acts. Naturally, therefore, we call neither horse nor ox nor any other of the brute beasts 'happy,' for none of them can have a share in such activity. This too is why a boy is not happy, for he is not capable of such acts owing to his age; those boys whom we do describe as happy are being cried up on account of the hopes we have of them. For there is required, as we said, goodness fully developed in a complete life, because many changes and all sorts of chances occur in life, and even the most flourishing may be the victim of grave misfortune in old age, as is told of Priam in the Trojan Cycle; and no one calls a man happy who has experienced such chances and ended in disaster.

7. CAN A MAN BE CALLED HAPPY WHILE HE LIVES?

We may ask then whether anyone at all is to be called happy while he lives. Must we, in Solon's words, first 'see the end'? Even if we are to admit this proposition, is it a fact that a man *is* happy *after he has died?* Is not such a statement utterly absurd, especially coming from us who maintain that happiness is an *activity?* On the other hand, if we do not describe the dead man as happy, and interpret Solon as meaning no more than that one can then (and not till then) safely *call* a man blessed as being at last beyond the reach of evil and misfortune, this also is open to question. For according to popular belief both evil and good exist to some extent for a dead man, just as much and just as little as for one who is alive but unaware of them; such things, I mean, as honour and dishonour and the good or bad fortune of children and of descendants generally. This too raises a problem; for although a man has lived happily into old age and died in a manner consistent with his life, his descendants may suffer many reverses. Some of them may be good and attain the life they deserve, while just the opposite happens to others. It is also clear that the degrees of relationship between them and their ancestors may vary indefinitely. It would be strange indeed if the dead man were to share in these variations, becoming now happy and now wretched; but it would also be strange if the fortunes of descendants did not, at any rate for some period and to some degree, affect the happiness of their ancestors.

However, let us return to our first problem, for its consideration may perhaps solve our present difficulty. If we must first 'see the end' and only then call a man happy, not as *being* happy but as *having been* so, surely it is absurd that when he *is* happy the attribute which he *here and now* possesses should not be truly predicated of him because of our unwillingness to call living men happy, owing to the vicissitudes to which they are subject, and because we have assumed happiness to be something permanent and by no means easily changed, whereas the living are at the mercy of Fortune's oft-turning wheel.

For clearly if we were to follow up a given man's fortunes, we should frequently call him at one time happy and at another miserable, pointing to the happy man as a 'chameleon changing colour to match its surroundings.' Or is it perhaps quite wrong thus to follow up his fortunes? Success or failure does not reside in these; human life, as we said a little while ago, has need of them as mere additions, whereas virtuous activities or their opposites are what constitute happiness or its reverse.

The problem we have just discussed bears witness to our definition. In no human function do we find such permanence as in virtuous activities;[1] and among virtuous activities the most honourable are the most permanent, because in them those who are happy spend their lives most willingly and most perseveringly.[2] Permanence, therefore, will belong to the happy man, and he will be happy throughout his life; for he will always, or in preference to everything else, be engaged in virtuous action and contemplation, and he will bear the ups and downs of life most nobly and with perfect dignity, if he is 'truly good' and 'foursquare beyond reproach.'

Now many events, varying in importance, occur by chance. Small bits of good fortune or of its opposite clearly do not affect the balance of life on one side or the other. But numerous great events, if they turn out propitiously, will make life happier;[3] on the other hand, if they come to grief they will crush and maim happiness, for they are a vehicle of pain as well as an obstacle to many activities. Yet, even in these, fine character shines

[1] They are considered to be more lasting even than knowledge of the sciences.

[2] This is probably why such activities are not forgotten.

[3] For they themselves are by nature calculated to add beauty to life, and the use made of them may be noble and good.

through when a man endures many great misfortunes, not because he is insensible to pain but because of the nobility and greatness of his soul.

If activities are, as I was saying, the determinants of a happy or an unhappy life, no happy man can become miserable; for he will never do things that are detestable and mean. We think that he who is truly good and wise bears all the accidents of life with proper dignity and always makes the best of present circumstances, as a good general makes the most efficient use of his available forces and a good shoemaker makes the best possible footwear from the hides with which he is supplied; and so in the case of all other craftsmen. And if this is so, the happy man can never become miserable, though he will never, of course, become *blessed* if he meet with fortunes like those of Priam.

Nor, again, is he many-coloured and changeable; for he will not be removed from his happy condition easily or by commonplace misfortunes, but only by many great ones. Nor, if he has suffered these latter, will he soon regain his happiness; if he does so at all it will be after a long period during which he will have achieved many notable successes.

What then is there to prevent our saying that he is happy who is active in accordance with complete virtue and is sufficiently equipped with external goods, not for any random length of time but throughout a complete life? Or must we add 'and who is destined to live thus and die a death consistent with his life'? The future is indeed obscure to us, while we hold happiness to be an end and something altogether final. In that case we shall apply the term happy to those among the living in whom these conditions are, and are to be, fulfilled—and call them *happy men*. So much for these questions.

8. WHETHER THE FORTUNES OF THE LIVING AFFECT THE DEAD

That the fortunes of a man's descendants and of all his friends should have no effect whatever upon his happiness seems a very churlish view and one opposed to common opinion. But since the events of life are numerous and widely different among themselves, and since some concern us more closely than others, it seems a long if not endless task to discuss each of them in detail; so perhaps a general outline will suffice. Now just as some of a man's own misfortunes have a certain weight and influence upon life while others are, as it were, lighter, so also there are variations among the misfortunes of his friends taken as a whole, and it makes a difference whether these various sufferings afflict the living or the dead.[1] We must therefore allow for this difference too; or rather perhaps for the fact that there is some uncertainty as to whether the dead share in any good or evil. These considerations do suggest that if anything at all, good or evil, penetrates to them it must be something obscure and unimportant, either in itself or for them, or if not, at least it must be such in quantity and quality as not to render happy those who are not happy, nor to deprive the blessed of their blessedness. The good and ill fortune of friends, therefore, seem to affect the dead in some way, but in such a way and to such an extent as

---

[1] A far greater difference than whether lawless and terrible deeds in a tragedy are assumed to take place behind the scenes or are represented on the open stage.

neither to make the happy unhappy nor to produce any
such result.

9. WHETHER HAPPINESS HAS A RELATIVE OR AN ABSOLUTE VALUE

Having settled these questions, let us inquire whether
happiness is something praiseworthy or something precious; for clearly it is not a potentiality. Everything that
is praiseworthy seems to be praised in virtue of its possessing some quality and being related in some way to
something else; for we praise the just or brave man,
and in general both the good man and virtue itself, on
account of the actions and functions to which they give
rise, and we praise the strong man, the good runner and
so forth in virtue of his being of a certain kind and
related in some way to something good and important.
This is clear also from the praises of the gods; it strikes
us as absurd that the gods should be referred to our
standard, but this *is* done because praise, as we said,
involves a reference to something else. Yet if praise is due
to such things as we have described, then the best things
deserve not praise but something greater and better, as
is indeed obvious; for what we do to the gods and the
most godlike of men is to call them blessed and happy.
And so also with good things; no one praises happiness as
he does justice; rather he calls it blessed, as something
more godlike and better.

Eudoxus, too, seems to have made an able plea in
support of pleasure's claim to the prize of highest excellence. He thought that the fact of its not being praised,
although it is a good, pointed to its being better than the
things that *are* praised, and that this is what God and
the Good are; for all else is judged by reference to these.

Praise is appropriate to *virtue,* for as a result of it men tend to perform noble deeds; but encomia are the rewards of *acts* both of the body and of the soul. But perhaps precision in these matters is more likely to be found among those who have made a careful study of encomia; to us it is clear from what has been said that happiness is among things precious and perfect. This is confirmed by the fact that happiness is a first principle; for it is with a view to this that all of us do whatever we do, and we account the first principle or cause of all goods as something precious and divine.

A. KINDS OF VIRTUE

SINCE happiness is an activity of soul in accordance with perfect virtue, we have to consider the nature of virtue, and thereby perhaps obtain a more distinct view of the nature of happiness. The true student of social science, too, is considered to have studied virtue above all else, for he seeks to make his fellow citizens good and obedient to the laws;[1] and if his quest belongs to social science, clearly some discussion of the nature of virtue will accord with our original plan. Now the virtue which we have to study is of course *human* virtue, since the good we are looking for is human good, and the happiness human happiness. By human virtue we mean not that of the body but that of the soul, and happiness also we describe as an activity of soul. Well, if this is so, clearly the student of social science needs to know something about soul, just as a man who proposes to heal the eyes or the body as a whole requires some knowledge of the eyes or of the body. His need is indeed proportionately greater as social science is more precious and better than medicine, though even among doctors physiologists are at great pains to understand the theory of the body. The student of social science, therefore, must study the soul. He must do so with a view to these objects, and to the exact extent sufficient for the questions we are discussing; a greater degree of precision calls, I think, for more trouble than our purposes demand.

Some aspects of the soul are adequately dealt with in

[1] As an example we have the Cretan and Spartan legislators, and any others of the kind there may have been.

writings extraneous to our school; we must make use of what they have to say, e.g. that one element of the soul is irrational while one has a rational principle. Whether these are separated as are the parts of the body or anything else divisible, or are two by definition but by nature inseparable (like convex and concave in the circumference of a circle), is irrelevant to the problem now before us.

One division of the irrational element appears to be widely distributed and vegetative in its nature, I mean that which is the cause of nutrition and growth. It is this kind of power of the soul that we must attribute to all organisms maintained by nutrition and to embryos, and it is more reasonable to assign this same power rather than some other to fully developed animals. Now the excellence of this power is seen to be common to all species and not exclusively to mankind; for the nutritive faculty seems to be peculiarly active in sleep, wherein goodness and badness are least apparent[1]—unless perhaps some of the motions of the senses actually penetrate a little into the soul, and in this respect the dreams of good men are better than those of bad men. But enough of this subject; let us leave the vegetative faculty, since it is by nature devoid of any share in human excellence as such.

There seems, however, to be another division of the irrational element, but one which has some kind of share in a rational principle. For we admire the rational principle both of the continent and of the self-indulgent man,

[1] Hence the saying that the happy are no better off than the wretched during half their lives. There is a deal of sound sense in that, because sleep is an inactivity of the soul, whereas the soul is called good or bad in respect of activity.

together with that element of their souls which possesses
such a principle, since it urges them aright and towards
the best objects. But we find in them also another element
by its nature opposed to the rational principle, which
fights and resists that principle. Exactly as paralysed
limbs when we decide to move them to the right turn
contrariwise to the left, so the impulses of a self-indulgent
man's soul move in opposition to the rational principle.
While we *see* what goes astray in bodies, in the soul we
do not; none the less we must undoubtedly suppose that
there is in the soul too something contrary to the rational
principle, opposing and resisting it. In what way it is
distinct from the other elements is none of our concern.
Now, as we said, even this seems to share in a rational
principle. At all events it obeys the rational principle
in the continent man; and presumably it is still more
obedient in the temperate and brave man, for in him it is
in complete harmony with the rational principle.

The irrational element then appears to be twofold.
While the vegetative division has no share whatever in a
rational principle, the appetitive and in general the
orectic division does in a sense have such a share, to the
extent that it listens to and obeys that principle. It is in
this sense that we speak of 'taking account' of one's father
and friends, not in the sense of 'accounting' for mathemat-
ical properties. That the irrational element is in some
sense governed by the rational principle is likewise shown
by the giving of advice and by every form of reproof
and exhortation. But if this orectic division of the irrational element must be said to have a rational principle,
that which has a rational principle will itself split up into
two, one division having it in the strict sense and in it-

self, the other having a tendency to obey as a man does his father.

Virtue likewise is divided into kinds in accordance with this difference. We say that some of the virtues are intellectual and others moral; philosophical wisdom and understanding and practical wisdom are intellectual, liberality and temperance moral. For when speaking of a man's character we do not say that he is wise or understanding, but that he is good-tempered or temperate; yet we praise the wise man also with respect to his disposition, and we call those dispositions which deserve praise 'virtues.'

Two Kinds   Virtues

Mor

VII The Ideal Life

A. PLEASURE

1. TWO VIEWS OF PLEASURE

OUR next task, I think, is to discuss pleasure. For it is considered to be intimately bound up with human nature, and this accounts for the fact that in educating the young we steer them by the rudders of pleasure and pain. It is also believed that excellence of character is determined to a very great extent by our enjoying and detesting what we ought. These actions extend throughout life, having a weight and power in respect both of virtue and of the happy life, since men choose what is pleasant and avoid what is painful. Such matters are surely the very last we should fail to discuss, especially as they are the subject of much debate.

Some say pleasure is the highest good, while others maintain that it is thoroughly bad. Some of the latter no doubt are persuaded that the facts are as they declare, whereas others think that our life is improved by the representation of pleasure as a bad thing even if it is not.[1] But surely this is not correct. Arguments about matters concerned with feelings and actions are less cogent than facts; and therefore when they are at variance with the facts of perception they are despised and bring the truth into discredit as well. If a man who cries out against pleasure is once seen to be aiming at it, his inclination towards it is taken to imply that it is wholly good, for most

[1] Most people, they think, incline towards it and are the slaves of their pleasures, for which reason they should be led in the opposite direction, and thus attain the middle state.

people are incapable of drawing distinctions. True arguments then seem most useful, not only with a view to knowledge, but with a view to life also; for since they harmonize with the facts they are believed, and so they stimulate those who understand them to live accordingly. But enough of these questions; let us go on to consider the opinions that have been expressed on the subject of pleasure.

2. THE OPINION THAT PLEASURE IS THE GOOD

Eudoxus thought pleasure to be the Good because he saw 'all things, rational and irrational, aiming at it,' and because the object of choice is invariably what is excellent, and that which is the principal object of choice the greatest good. Thus the fact that all things 'moved towards the same object' suggested to him that this object was for all things the chief good,[1] and that that which was good for all things and at which all aimed was *the* Good. His arguments were credited not so much for their own worth as for the excellence of his character; he appeared to have exceptional control of himself, and so it was thought that he was not expressing himself merely as a friend of pleasure but in accordance with the facts. He believed the same conclusion to follow no less clearly from a study of pain, the opposite of pleasure; pain was in itself an object of universal abhorrence, and therefore its opposite must be likewise an object of choice. Again, that is most of all an object of choice which we choose not because or for the sake of something else; now pleasure is admittedly of this nature, for no one asks to what end he is pleased, thus implying that pleasure is in

[1] For each thing, he argued, finds its own good as it finds its own nourishment.

itself an object of choice. Further, he argued that pleasure when added to any good, e.g. to just or temperate action, makes it more worthy of choice, and that it is only by itself that good can be increased.

This last argument seems to show pleasure to be one good among many, and no more a good than any of the others; for every good is more worthy of choice when taken along with another good than alone. And so it is by an argument of this kind that Plato proves that pleasure is *not* the Good; he argues that the pleasant life is more desirable with practical wisdom than without, and that if the mixture is better, pleasure is not the Good; for the Good cannot become more desirable by the addition of anything that is good in itself. What then is there that satisfies this criterion and can be reconciled with our own view? We are looking for something of this sort.

Those who object that that at which all things aim is not necessarily good are, of course, talking nonsense. For we say that what *everyone* thinks really is *as* they think; and anyone who assails this belief will scarcely be able to substitute a more credible opinion. In so far as creatures devoid of intelligence desire the things in question, there might be something in what they say; but in so far as intelligent creatures do the same, what sense can there be in this view? Perhaps even in inferior creatures there is something stronger than themselves which aims at their proper good.

Nor does the argument about the contrary of pleasure appear to be sound. It is said that if pain is an evil it does not follow that pleasure is a good, for evil is opposed to evil and at the same time both are opposed to the neutral state. This is correct enough, but does not apply here. If both pleasure and pain were evils, they ought both to be objects of aversion, while that which is neutral ought to be neither shunned nor sought, or both alike. In fact, however, the one is manifestly avoided as evil and the other chosen as good, so the antithesis is of this kind.

3. THE OPINION THAT PLEASURE IS WHOLLY BAD

Nor again, if pleasure is not a quality, does it follow that it is not a good; for the activities of virtue are not qualities either, nor is happiness.

They say, however, that the Good is determinate, whereas pleasure is indeterminate; because it admits of degrees. Now if it is from the feeling of pleasure that their judgment is derived, the same will be true of justice and the other virtues, in respect of which we say unhesitatingly that people of a certain character possess that character to a greater or less degree and act more or less in accordance with those virtues; for a man may be more just or more courageous, and it is possible also to act more or less justly and temperately. But if their judgment is based on the various pleasures, surely they are failing to state the cause of the badness of some pleasures, if in fact some pleasures are unmixed and others mixed? Again, just as health admits of degrees without being indeterminate, what is there to prevent pleasure doing likewise? The same proportion is not found in all things, nor a single proportion always in the same thing; it may be diminished and yet persist up to a point,[1] and it may differ in degree. The case of pleasure too may therefore be of this sort.

---

[1] There is always some latitude in a mean state. It is impossible, for instance, to distinguish very small musical intervals; so a note may be sharp or flat and remain, so far as we are concerned, the same note.

Moreover they assume that the Good is perfect while movements and comings into being are imperfect, and they try to exhibit pleasure as (*a*) a movement and (*b*) a coming into being. But (*a*) they do not appear to be right even in saying that it is a movement. For rapidity or slowness are considered to be proper to every movement, and if a movement, e.g. that of the first heaven, has not rapidity or slowness in itself, it has it in relation to something else.[1] But neither of these things is true of pleasure. For while we may *become* pleased quickly, as we may become angry quickly, we cannot *be* pleased quickly, not even in relation to someone else, whereas we *can* walk, grow, etc., quickly. While then we can change quickly or slowly into a pleasurable state, we cannot quickly exhibit the activity of pleasure, i.e. *be pleased*. Again, (*b*) how can pleasure be a coming into being? It is held that no chance thing can come out of any chance thing, but that a thing is dissolved into that from which it comes into being;[2] and pain would be the dissolution of that of which pleasure is the coming into being.

It is also maintained that pain is the lack of that which is according to nature, and that pleasure is replenishment. But these affections are bodily. If then pleasure is replenishment with that which is according to nature, that which feels pleasure will be that in which the replenishment

[1] [Aristotle means that since the circular motion of the first heaven (the fixed stars) has no acceleration or retardation we cannot call it rapid or slow *in itself*, for there is no quicker or slower motion of itself with which to compare it. But if it be compared with the derivative motions like that of the planets we can call it rapid.]

[2] [A thing can only become actually what it is potentially, since coming into being is the process towards actuality of the form contained potentially in a thing. The reverse process is determined in the same way.]

takes place, i.e. the body. But this seems not to be the case; therefore the replenishment is not pleasure, although one would be pleased while replenishment was in progress, just as one would be pained during a surgical operation.[1] This opinion seems to be derived from the pains and pleasures connected with nutrition; from the fact that when a man has suffered the pangs of hunger he is pleased with the replenishment. But this does not happen with all pleasures; the pleasures of learning and, among sensuous pleasures, those of smell, and also many sounds and sights, and memories and hopes, do not presuppose pain. Of what then will these be the coming into being? There has been no lack of anything of which they could be the replenishment.

To those who bring forward the culpable pleasures one may reply that these are not by nature pleasant at all; if things are pleasant to persons of evil disposition, we must not suppose that they are pleasant to others, any more than we suppose that things wholesome or sweet or bitter to the sick are so to people in good health, or than we ascribe whiteness to things that seem white to persons with defective eyesight. Or again one might answer as follows; pleasures are desirable, but not from these particular sources; as wealth is desirable, but not as the price of betrayal; and health too, but not upon condition of eating anything and everything. Or yet again, perhaps: pleasures differ in kind; those derived from honourable sources are different from those derived from shameful sources, and one cannot enjoy the pleasure of a just man without being just, nor that of a musical man without being musical, and so forth.

[1] [Aristotle's meaning here is that the being replenished no more *is* pleasure than the being operated upon *is* pain.]

The fact, moreover, that a friend is different from a flatterer seems to make it clear that pleasure is not a good or that pleasures differ in kind; for the friend is said to consort with us with a view to the good, the flatterer with a view to our pleasure, and the latter is reproached for his conduct while the former is praised on the ground that he consorts with us for different purposes. That pleasures differ in kind is indicated also by the fact that no one would choose to live with the intelligence of a child throughout his life, no matter how much he were to take pleasure in the things that delight children; and also by the fact that no one would choose to obtain enjoyment by doing something utterly disgraceful, even if it were to involve him in no pain at all. And there are many things we would be keen to do, even if they brought no pleasure in their train, e.g. seeing, remembering, knowing, possessing the virtues. It makes no difference that these are necessarily accompanied by pleasure; we would choose them even if no pleasure resulted from our doing so. It seems to be clear then that pleasure is not the Good, that not all pleasure is desirable, and that some pleasures are desirable in themselves, differing from the rest in kind or in their sources. So much for the several opinions as to pleasure and pain.

4. DEFINITION OF PLEASURE

What pleasure is, or what kind of thing it is, will become clearer if we take up the question again from the beginning. Seeing appears to be at any given moment complete, for it does not lack anything which must come into being later and complete its form. Pleasure also seems to be of this nature; for it is a whole, and at no time can one find a pleasure whose form will be com-

pleted if the pleasure lasts longer. Hence too it is not a
movement; for every movement (e.g. that of building)
takes time and is directed to some end, and is complete
when it has produced what it aims at. It is complete
therefore only in the whole time it takes or in the instant
that it attains its end. In their parts, i.e. the successive
stages leading to the end, all movements are incomplete,
and are different in kind from the whole movement and
from each other. The fitting together of the stones is
different from the fluting of the column, and these are
both different from the construction of the temple as a
whole. And the construction of the temple as a whole is
complete (since it lacks nothing with a view to the task
in hand); but the construction of the base or of the tri-
glyph is incomplete, for each is the construction of only a
part. Consequently they differ in kind, and it is not possible to find at any and every period of time a movement
complete in form, but, if at all, only in the *whole* time.
So also in the case of walking and all other movements.
For if locomotion is a movement from one point to another, it too has differences in kind: flying, walking and
running, jumping and so forth. Moreover even in walking
and running such differences are present; for the *terminus
a quo* and the *terminus ad quem* are not the same in the
whole racecourse as in part of it, nor in one part as in
another; nor is it the same thing to cross line A as to cross
line B, for one crosses not only a line but one which is in a
place, and B is in a different place from A.[1] We have
discussed movement in detail elsewhere; it seems that it

[1] [If one draws a number of lines across a racecourse, the crossing of each successive line brings the process of running nearer
completion. The crossing of each is specifically different; for the
differentia of locomotion is 'whence—whither,' and the lines differ
in this respect.]

is not complete at any and every moment but that the many movements into which it may be divided are incomplete and different in kind, since the whence and whither give them their form. The form of pleasure, on the other hand, *is* complete at any and every period of time. Clearly then pleasure and movement must be different from one another, and pleasure must be one of the things that are whole and complete. This is shown also by the fact that it is not possible to move otherwise than in time, but it *is* possible to be thus pleased; for that which takes place in a moment is a whole.

From these considerations it is also clear that one cannot rightly say there is a movement or coming into being *of* pleasure. For these cannot be predicated of all things, but only of those that are divisible, i.e. not wholes; there is no coming into being of seeing nor of a point nor of a unit, nor is any of these a movement or a coming into being. Therefore there is no movement or coming into being of pleasure either, because it is a whole.

Since every sense is active in relation to its object, and a sense in good condition acts perfectly in relation to the most beautiful of its objects,[1] it follows that in the case of each sense the best activity is that of the best-conditioned organ in relation to the noblest of its objects. And this activity will be the most complete and the most pleasant. For although there is pleasure in respect of every sense, and in respect of thought and contemplation likewise, the most complete is the most pleasant, and that of a well-conditioned organ in relation to the finest of its objects is the most complete; and the pleasure of its

[1] For perfect activity seems to be ideally of such a nature; whether we say that *it* is active, or the organ in which it resides may be considered immaterial.

objects is activity. But the pleasure does not complete it in the same way as does the combination of object and sense, both of them being good, just as health and the doctor are not in the same way the cause[1] of a man's being healthy.[2] Pleasure completes the activity not as does its immanent formal cause, but as a superadded perfection, as the bloom of youth completes those in the flower of life. Provided therefore that both the intelligible or sensible object and the discriminating or contemplative faculty are as they should be, the pleasure will be present in the activity; for when both the passive and the passive factors are alike and similarly related to one another, the same result naturally follows.

How then comes it that no one is continuously pleased? Because we grow weary? It is at any rate a fact that no human being is capable of continuous activity. Therefore pleasure also is not continuous, for it accompanies activity. Some things delight us when they are new, but afterwards do so less, for the same reason; at first the mind is stirred up and is intensely active with regard to them (as when people *look* and do not merely *see*), but afterwards its activity is not of this kind, but has become relaxed, and hence the pleasure too is dimmed.

One might think that all men desire pleasures because they all aim at life. Life is an activity, and every man is

[1] [The object and the doctor are efficient causes, sense and health formal causes.]

[2] It is clear that pleasure arises in respect of each sense, for we describe sights and sounds as pleasant. It is also plain that it arises principally when the sense is at its best and is active in reference to a corresponding object; when object and perceiver are at their best there will always be pleasure, since the requisite agent and patient are both present.

active about those things and with those faculties that he loves most,[1] but pleasure completes the activities, and therefore life, which they desire. It is with good reason then that they aim at pleasure too, since for every man it completes life, which is desirable. We may for the time being dismiss the question whether we choose life for the sake of pleasure or *vice versa*. For both appear to interlock and not to admit of separation, since pleasure does not arise without activity, and every activity is completed by the accompanying pleasure.

5. HOW PLEASURES DIFFER, AND WHAT IS THE NORM OF THEIR VALUE

For the above reason pleasures appear also to differ in kind. We think that things different in kind are completed by things differing in kind. Now the activities of thought differ in kind from the senses, and these in turn differ likewise among themselves; so, therefore, do the pleasures that complete them.

The same is evident from the fact that each of the pleasures is bound up with the activity it completes. For an activity is intensified by its proper pleasure, since each class of things is better judged of and reduced to precision by those who engage in the activity with pleasure; e.g. it is those who enjoy geometrical procedure that become geometers and obtain a better grasp of the various propositions, and similarly those who are fond of music or of building and so forth[2] make progress in their proper function by enjoying it. So the pleasures intensify the

[1] The musician, for example, is active with his hearing about melodies, the student with his mind about theoretical questions, and so on.

[2] This is manifestly true both of natural objects and of artifacts, e.g. animals, trees, a painting, a statue, a house, a tool.

activities, and what intensifies a thing is proper to it, but things different in kind have properties different in kind.

This will be even more evident from the fact that activities are hindered by pleasures arising from elsewhere. People who are fond of playing the flute are no longer capable of attending to an argument if they happen to hear someone playing the flute, for they enjoy flute-playing more than the activity in progress; so the pleasure connected with flute-playing destroys the activity concerned with argument. This happens, similarly, in all other cases when a man is active about two things at the same time; the more pleasant activity launches an attack upon the other, and all the more furiously if it is *much* more pleasant, even to the extent of destroying it altogether. This is why when we enjoy something very much we are not greatly interested in anything else, and do one thing only when we are not much pleased by another. In the theatre, for instance, those who eat sweets do so mostly when the acting is poor. Now since activities are rendered keener, more lasting and better by their proper pleasure, and damaged by alien pleasures, the two kinds of pleasure are obviously far removed from one another. For alien pleasures do more or less what proper pains do, since activities are destroyed by their proper pains. Thus if a man finds writing or making calculations unpleasant and painful, he refrains from writing, or from making calculations, because the activity is painful. An activity therefore suffers contrary effects from its proper pleasures and pains, i.e. from those which supervene upon it by virtue of its own nature. And we have said that alien pleasures do much the same as pain; they destroy the activity, though not to the same extent.

Now since activities differ in respect of goodness and

badness, and some are worthy of choice, others of avoid-
ance and others again neutral, so too are the pleasures; for
every activity has its own peculiar pleasure. The pleasure
proper to a virtuous activity is good, and that proper to
an unworthy activity bad; just as the appetites for noble
objects are praiseworthy, and those for base objects repre-
hensible. But the pleasures involved in activities are more
proper to them than the desires from which they arise; for
the latter are antecedent in time to and different in nature
from the activities, while the pleasures are so close to and
so hard to distinguish from them as to raise a doubt
whether the activity is not the same as the pleasure.[1] Well
then, just as activities are different so are the corresponding pleasures. Now sight is superior to touch in purity,
and hearing and smell to taste; the corresponding pleasures therefore are likewise superior, and those of thought
superior to these, and within each of the two kinds some
are superior to others.

Every animal is thought to have a proper pleasure as
it has a proper function—the pleasure, namely, which
corresponds to its activity. This will also be evident if we
survey them species by species. Horse, dog and man
have different pleasures; as Heraclitus says, 'Asses would
prefer hay to gold,' for food is more pleasant than gold
to asses. So the pleasures of creatures different in kind
are themselves different in kind, and it is reasonable to
assume that those of a single species do not differ in this
way. But they do vary to no small extent, in the case of
human beings at any rate; the same things delight some
people and pain others, and are painful and odious to

[1] Pleasure of course is not really thought or perception—that
would be odd; but it *appears* to some people the same because it
is never found apart from one or other of them.

some, but pleasant to and liked by others. This happens too in the case of sweet things; the same things do not seem sweet to a man in the grip of fever and to one in good health, nor hot to a weak man and to one in good condition, and so forth. But in all such matters that which appears to the good man is considered to be really so. If this view is correct, as it seems to be, and virtue and the good man as such are the measure of each thing, it follows that whatever appears to him as a pleasure will really be a pleasure, and that whatever he enjoys will really be pleasant. Do not be surprised if what he dislikes seems pleasant to someone else, for men may be ruined or damaged in many ways; what he dislikes is not *really* pleasant, but only to this someone else, i.e. to one who has been in some way ruined or damaged. Pleasures that are admittedly shameful should not be described as pleasures at all, except to a perverted taste; but as regards those that are considered good, what kind of pleasure or what individual pleasure should we say is proper to man? Is it not plain from the corresponding activities? The pleasures follow these. Accordingly, whether the perfect and supremely happy man has one or more activities, the pleasures that perfect it or them may be said in the strict sense to be pleasures proper to man, and the rest will be so in a secondary and even a far lower degree, as are the activities.

1. HAPPINESS IS NOT AMUSEMENT, BUT
GOOD ACTIVITY

HAVING discussed the virtues, the forms of friendship and the varieties of pleasure, we are left with the task of outlining the nature of happiness, which is what we claim the end of human nature to be. Our discussion will be more concise if we begin by summarizing what has already been said. We have explained that happiness is not a disposition; otherwise it might reside in someone who was asleep or merely vegetated during the whole of his life, or again in someone who was suffering the worst misfortunes. If these implications are unacceptable, and we must rather classify happiness as an activity, as we said earlier on, and if (a) some activities are necessary, and desirable for the sake of something else, while (b) others are so in themselves, then happiness must obviously be placed in group (b), not in (a); for happiness lacks nothing, but is self-sufficient. Now those activities are desirable in themselves from which nothing is sought other than the activity; and virtuous actions are regarded as being of this nature, for to do good and noble deeds is a thing desirable for its own sake.

Pleasant amusements also are considered to be of this nature; we do not choose them for the sake of other things, for since they lead us to neglect our bodies and our property they injure rather than benefit us. But most of the people who are looked upon as happy take refuge in such pastimes, and that is why those who are adepts therein enjoy great esteem at the court of a tyrant; they make themselves pleasant companions in the tyrant's favourite pursuits, and that is the sort of man your tyrant always wants. Now these pleasant amusements are thought to be of the nature of happiness because people in high places devote their leisure to them. But surely such people are of no significance. After all, virtue and reason, from which good activities proceed, do not depend upon exalted position. Besides, these people have never tasted pure and generous pleasure, so if they take refuge in physical pleasures the latter should not for that reason be considered more desirable; boys too are in the habit of believing that what is esteemed among themselves is automatically the best. It is therefore to be expected that, as different things are held in honour by boys and by grown men, so they should be by bad men and by good. Now, as we have often said, those things are both estimable and pleasant which are such to the good man; and to each man the activity in accordance with his own disposition is most desirable, and, therefore, to the good man that which is in accordance with virtue. Consequently happiness is not to be found in amusement; it would indeed be strange if the end were amusement, and one were to take trouble and endure hardships all one's life in order to amuse oneself. For, in a word, everything that we choose we choose for the sake of something else —except happiness, which is the end. Now to exert oneself and work for the sake of amusement seems silly and indeed utterly childish. But to amuse oneself in order that one may exert oneself, as Anacharsis says, seems right; for amusement is a sort of relaxation, and we need relaxation because we cannot work continuously. Relaxation then is not the end; it is taken for the sake of activity.

The happy life is thought to be virtuous; but a virtuous life demands exertion, and noes not consist in amusement.

And we say that serious things are better than ludicrous things and those connected with amusement, and that the activity of the better of two things—whether two elements of our own being or two men—is the more serious; but the activity of the better is *ipso facto* superior and more of the nature of happiness. Again, any chance person, even a slave, can enjoy physical pleasures no less than the best of men; but no one allows that a slave has any share in happiness, unless he also allows that a slave has some share in human life. For happiness is not to be found in physical pleasures, but, as we said before, in virtuous activities.

2. HAPPINESS IN THE HIGHEST SENSE IS THE CONTEMPLATIVE LIFE

If happiness is activity in accordance with virtue, it may reasonably be taken to be in accordance with the highest virtue; and this activity will be that of the best thing in us. Whether reason or something else is this element which is thought to be our natural ruler and to guide and to take thought of things noble or divine, whether it be itself also divine or only the most nearly divine element in us, its activity in accordance with its proper virtue will be perfect happiness. We have already explained that such activity is contemplation.

Now this would seem to agree both with our earlier remarks and with the truth. For this activity is (*a*) the best, since not only is reason the best thing in us, but the objects of reason are the best of knowable objects; and it is (*b*) the most continuous, since we can contemplate more continuously than we can *do* anything. Further, we think pleasure to be bound up with happiness, but the activity of theoretical wisdom is admittedly the most pleas-

ant of virtuous activities; at any rate its pursuit is believed to entail pleasures wonderful for their purity and
for the way they endure, and it is only natural that those
who know should pass their time more pleasantly than
those who are still inquiring. Again, what we have called
self-sufficiency must belong principally to the contemplative activity. For whereas the philosopher, as well as the
just man or one possessing any other virtue, requires the
necessaries of life, once they are sufficiently endowed
therewith, the just, temperate or brave man still needs
people towards whom and with whom he may act justly,
temperately or bravely, but the philosopher can contemplate truth even when all alone, and can contemplate it
the better in proportion to his degree of wisdom; he can
perhaps do so even better if he has fellow workers, but
still he is the most self-sufficient. And this activity alone
would seem to be loved for its own sake; for nothing
arises from it apart from contemplation, whereas from
practical activities we derive much or little apart from the
action. Happiness, moreover, is thought to depend on
leisure; for we busy ourselves that we may have leisure,
and make war that we may live in peace. Now the activity
of the practical virtues is exhibited in political or military
affairs, but the actions concerned with these seem to be
unleisurely. Warlike actions are completely so. No one
chooses to be at war or prepares for war merely in order
to be at war; anyone who made enemies of his friends in
order to precipitate battle and slaughter would seem nothing short of a murderer. But the statesman's action is
also unleisurely; apart from the political action itself, it
aims at despotic power and honours, or anyhow at happiness for himself and his fellow citizens—a happiness
different from political action and sought as being differ-

ent. If therefore among virtuous actions (*a*) political and military actions are distinguished by nobility and greatness, being at the same time unleisurely, aiming at an end distinct from themselves, and therefore not desirable for their own sake, but (*b*) the contemplative activity of reason seems both to be superior in serious worth and to aim at no end beyond itself, and to have its proper pleasure (which increases the activity), and (*c*) the self-sufficiency, leisureliness, unweariedness (so far as this is possible for human beings) and all the other attributes ascribed to the supremely happy man are evidently those connected with the contemplative activity of reason, it follows that this will be man's complete happiness—if it be allowed a complete term of life, for none of the attributes of happiness is *in*complete.

Such a life, however, would be too exalted for mere man. It is not *qua* man that he will live thus, but in so far as something divine is present in him; and according as the divine something is superior to our composite nature, so its activity is superior to that which is the exercise of the other kind of virtue. If then reason is divine in comparison with man, the life according to reason is divine in comparison with human life. But we must not listen to those who assure us that 'being men we should think on human things' or that 'being mortals we should dwell upon mortal things.' No, so far as possible we must make ourselves immortal, and exert ourselves to live in accordance with what is best in us; for even though it be, so to speak, small in bulk, it far surpasses everything else in power and worth. This 'best thing in us,' too, would seem to be each man himself, since it is the authoritative and better part of him. It would be absurd then if he were to choose not the life of his self but that of something else. What we said earlier is applicable here: that which is proper to each thing is by nature best and most pleasant for each; consequently for man the life according to reason is best and most pleasant, since reason more than anything else *is* man. This life therefore is also the happiest.

The life in accordance with moral virtue is happy in a secondary degree; for the activities in accordance with such virtue befit our human state. We do just, brave and other virtuous acts in relation to one another, fulfilling our respective duties in the matter of contracts, services and all sorts of practical affairs, and also with regard to the passions, all of which are recognized as typically human. Some of them appear even to arise from the body, and excellence of character to be in many ways bound up with the passions. Practical wisdom too is connected with excellence of character, and *vice versa,* since the principles of practical wisdom are in accordance with the moral virtues and rightness of morals is in accordance with practical wisdom. Being connected with the passions also, the moral virtues must belong to our composite nature. But the virtues of the latter are human; so, therefore, are the life and the happiness which correspond to these. The excellence of the reason is a thing apart; that statement must suffice, for to describe it in detail is a task beyond the scope of our present inquiry. We may, however, observe that it seems to have little need of external equipment, less at any rate than moral virtue has. Both, it is true, stand in equal need of the necessities of life, even though the statesman's work is more concerned with the body; in this respect there is little difference between them, but there will be a great difference in what they need for the exercise of their respective activities. The liberal man will need money for the exercise of his liberality, and the just man too in order to pay for services rendered;[1] and the brave man will need power if he is to perform any of the deeds corresponding to his particular virtue; and the temperate man will need opportunity, otherwise how is he (or indeed any of the others just mentioned) to be recognized? It is debated also whether the will or the deed is more essential to virtue, which is assumed to involve both. It is surely clear that its perfection *does* involve both; but many things are required for deeds, and all the more things according as those deeds are greater and nobler. A man who is contemplating truth, on the other hand, needs no such things, at any rate with a view to the exercise of his activity; indeed one might even describe them as obstacles to his contemplation. But in so far as he is a man living in society he chooses to do virtuous acts, and will consequently need such aids to living a human life.

The following consideration also will show that perfect happiness is a contemplative activity. We suppose the gods to be blessed and happy above all other things; but what sort of actions must be assigned to them? Acts of justice? Surely it is absurd to think of the gods as making contracts, returning deposits and so forth. Acts of courage then, as when a brave man confronts danger and runs risks because it is noble to do so? Ridiculous! Liberal acts? To whom will they give? It is laughable to think of them as handling money or anything like that. And what would their temperate acts be? To praise them for the performance of such is an insult, since they have no bad appetites. If we were to enumerate every kind of virtue,

[1] Wishes are obscure, and even people who are not just pretend to wish to act justly.

the circumstances of their exercise would be found trivial and unworthy of gods. All the same, everyone assumes that they *live* and therefore that they are active; we cannot suppose them to be asleep like Endymion. Now if you take away action (especially productive action) from a living being, what is left? Why, contemplation. Therefore the activity of God, which excels all others in blessedness, must be contemplative; and consequently the human activity most akin to His must be most of the nature of happiness.

Yet another indication of this is the fact that brute beasts have no share in happiness; they are utterly devoid of such activity. For while the whole life of the gods is supremely happy, and that of men too in so far as some likeness of the divine activity pertains to them, none of the other animals is happy, since they have absolutely no share in contemplation. Happiness then is co-extensive with contemplation, and those to whom contemplation belongs more fully are more truly happy, not just incidentally but by virtue of their contemplation which is precious in itself. Happiness therefore must be some form of contemplation.

But a man, precisely because he is a man, will also need external well-being in order to be happy. Our nature is not self-sufficient for the purpose of contemplation; our bodies too must be healthy and must have access to food and other care. Nevertheless we must not imagine that a man who is to be happy will need many things or great things, merely because he cannot be supremely happy without external goods; for self-sufficiency and action do not involve excess. One can perform noble actions without ruling land and sea; it is possible to act virtuously even with a moderate endowment of this world's goods,[1] and if one has that it is enough, for if a man is active in accordance with virtue his life will be happy. Solon too, I think, drew a fair portrait of the happy man when he described him as moderately equipped with external goods, but as having done the noblest acts and lived temperately; for one can do one's duty even with moderate possessions. Anaxagoras also seems to have supposed the happy man to be neither rich nor powerful; he said he would not be surprised if the happy man were to be looked upon by most people as rather an odd creature, since most people notice and judge by nothing but external appearances. Our arguments then seem to accord with the opinions of the sages; but while this fact carries a certain amount of weight, the truth in practical affairs must be discerned from the facts of life, which are in the last resort decisive. We must therefore survey what we have said up to this point, testing it by the facts of life; if it harmonizes with those facts it must be accepted, but if it is at variance with them it must be regarded as nothing more than theory.

3. CONCLUSION

Assuming now that happiness and the virtues, friendship and pleasure have all been sufficiently outlined, are we to suppose that our programme is concluded? No indeed; there is a saying that where you are dealing with things to be done the end is not to survey and recognize them, but rather to *do* them. With regard to virtue then, it is not enough to know all about it; we must try to possess and practise it, or make use of any other possible means of becoming good. If arguments were sufficient in

[1] This is perfectly clear, for private persons no less than rulers are considered to do good deeds—more so in fact.

themselves to make men good, they would justly, as Theognis says, have won many great rewards, and such rewards should have been conferred upon them. But as things are, while they seem able to encourage and stimulate the generous-minded among our youth, to form a gentlemanly character and a true lover of all that is honest and upright, ready to be possessed by virtue, they are *not* able to encourage the rank and file to lead noble and righteous lives. The ordinary run of men are not inclined by nature to obey the sense of shame, but only fear; they do not refrain from vicious conduct because of its baseness, but through fear of punishment. Living by passion they pursue their own pleasures and the means to them, avoid the opposite pains, and lack the very conception of what is noble and truly pleasant, having never tasted it. What argument could remould such people? It is difficult, if not impossible, to remove by argument what has long since been part and parcel of the character; we should perhaps think ourselves lucky if a combination of all the recognized means of acquiring virtue is effective.

Some take the view that we are rendered good by nature, others by habituation and others again by teaching. Nature's part is clearly independent of ourselves; thanks to some divine cause it is present in those who are truly fortunate. It is probable too that argument and teaching carry little weight with mankind as a whole; what is needed is the soul of a student trained to noble joy and noble hatred, like soil prepared for the nourishment of seed. A man who lives according to the dictates of passion will not listen to arguments intended to dissuade him from doing so, and even if he does he will not obey its voice; so the question arises how such a person can be persuaded to alter his course. You may take it as a general rule that passion yields not to argument but to compulsion; so what we need is a character predisposed to virtue, loving what is noble and hating what is base.

It is difficult, however, to be properly trained to virtue from youth upwards unless one has been brought up under right laws; for temperate and hardy living is not pleasant to most people, especially when they are young. Consequently our nurture and occupations should be regulated by laws, for they will not be irksome once we have grown used to them. But it is surely not enough that we should receive the right nurture and attention in childhood. Even when grown up we shall need to practise and be habituated to virtuous living, and therefore we shall need appropriate laws covering the whole of life; for most people bow to necessity sooner than to argument, to the threat of punishment rather than to the sense of what is noble.

Hence it is that some think legislators should exhort men to virtue and urge them forward with the motive of nobility, on the assumption that those who have been well advanced by the formation of habits will respond to such influences. They think too that penal sanctions should be applied to those who disobey and are of inferior nature, while the incurably bad should be banished from society altogether; they believe that since a good man lives with his mind fixed upon what is noble he will submit to argument, whereas a bad man, whose desire is for pleasure alone, is corrected by pain like a beast of burden. This, moreover, is the reason why they say that the pains inflicted on such men should be diametrically opposed to the pleasures which they love.

Be that as it may, if (*a*) we spoke the truth in saying that a man in order to be good must be trained to good habits, then go on to spend his time in worthy occupations and neither willingly nor unwillingly do bad actions, and if (*b*) this can be effected only by a man's living in accordance with some sort of reason and right order, provided this has force at its disposal, it follows that paternal authority lacks the requisite force or compulsive power.[1] But the law *has* this power, and it is at the same time a rule proceeding from a form of practical wisdom and reason. Besides, whereas people hate men who oppose their instincts, even though such opposition is fully justified, the law arouses no such feeling when it lays down what is good.

In the Spartan state alone, or almost alone, does the legislator seem to have dealt with questions of nurture and occupation; in most states such matters have been neglected, and each man lives as he pleases, Cyclops-fashion, 'dealing law to his own wife and children.'

It is best that such matters should be an official public concern; but if they are neglected by the community it would seem right for each man to help his children and friends towards virtue, and that they should have the power, or at least the will, to do this. It would seem from what we have said that the man most likely to be able to do this will be one who has been trained as a legislator. For public control is clearly effected by laws, and virtuous control by good laws; whether these are written or unwritten would seem to make no difference, nor whether they are laws providing for the education of individuals or of groups—any more than it does in the

[1] So too indeed does the authority of any individual, unless he be a king or hold some similar position.

case of music, or gymnastic or other such pursuits. Just as laws and predominant types of character are decisive in a city-state, so are the habits and directions of the father in a household. These habits and directions are in point of fact even more influential because of the bond of kinship and the benefits which he confers, for his offspring start with a natural affection and tendency to obey him. Futhermore private education has an advantage over public, as private medical treatment has. While rest and abstinence from food are generally speaking good for a man in the state of fever, they may not be so in a particular case; nor, presumably, does a boxer prescribe the same style of ring-craft for all his pupils. It would seem then that points of detail are worked out with greater precision if the control is private, for then each individual is likely to receive what is best adapted to his special circumstances.

On the other hand details can best be attended to by a doctor, a gymnastic instructor and so forth who possesses the general knowledge of what is good for everyone or for people of a certain kind. For the various sciences are rightly said to be concerned with universals; although of course some particular detail may be well looked after by an unscientific person, provided he has made a careful study of every set of circumstances in the light of experience, just as some men appear to be their own best doctors despite the fact that they could be of no assistance to anyone else. Nevertheless it will hardly be denied that if a man wishes to become master of an art or science he must go to the universal and get to know it as well as possible; for, as we have said, it is with the universal that sciences are concerned.

And surely a man who seeks to make others, be they

few or many, better by his care must try to become an adept in legislation, if laws are a means to our becoming good. For to take anyone whomsoever—anyone whom one happens to come across—and organize his life along the right lines is not anybody's job; it can be done only by one with the requisite knowledge, just as in medicine and other matters which give scope for care and prudence.

Undoubtedly then we must next try to discover by what means or from whom we may learn how to legislate. From statesmen, you may, since we found the art of legislation to be a part of political science; but one may ask whether any difference is apparent between statesmanship and the other sciences and arts. In the others the same people are found offering themselves as teachers and practising them, e.g. doctors and painters. But while the sophists profess to teach statesmanship, it is practised not by any of them but by men in public life, who would seem to do so by virtue of a certain skill and experience rather than of thought; for we do not find them either writing or lecturing about such matters[1] nor again do they appear to have made statesmen of their own sons or any of their friends. Yet surely one might expect them to do so if they were able; for they could bequeath to their respective states nothing better than such skill, nor could they desire anything better for themselves and for those dearest to them. Experience, however, seems to contribute not a little, otherwise they could not have become statesmen through familiarity with politics; and so it seems that those who aim at understanding the statesman's art need experience as well.

But those of the sophists who profess the art seem very

---

[1] Though to do so would perhaps be a more honourable occupation than writing speeches for the law-courts and the Ecclesia.

far from teaching it. For, to put the matter in a nutshell, they do not even know what kind of thing it is nor what it is all about; otherwise they would not have made it identical with rhetoric, nor have thought it easy to legislate by making a synthesis of reputable laws. They say it is possible to select the best laws, as though the very selection required no intelligence and as though right judgment were not the greatest thing, as for instance in music. While men experienced in any skill are sound judges of its products, understand from what materials and how the latter are produced, and what harmonizes with what, the inexperienced are lucky if they do not fail to see whether a work, e.g. a painting, has been well or badly made. Now laws are as it were the 'works' of statesmanship; how then can one learn from them to be a legislator, or judge which are the best? Even doctors do not seem to be formed by the study of medical books. There is such a thing as describing forms of treatment and the cures appropriate to given classes of treatment, distinguishing the various parts of the body; but while this seems useful to experienced men, it is valueless to the inexperienced. Surely then, while collections of laws and constitutions may be useful to those who can study them, judge what is good and bad and determine what enactments suit particular circumstances, those who peruse such collections without the necessary qualifications will not have sound judgment (except perhaps as a spontaneous gift of nature), though they may perhaps become more intelligent in such matters.

Now our predecessors have bequeathed to us the subject of legislation in an undeveloped state; it is right therefore that we ourselves should study it, and indeed the whole question of the constitution, in order to complete as best we may our philosophy of human nature. First then (*a*) let us try to review such intelligent observations as have come down to us from earlier thinkers; then (*b*) in the light of the constitutions we have collected let us study what kinds of influence preserve and destroy states and what kinds preserve or destroy particular types of constitution, and for what means some are well and others badly administered. When these have been examined we shall perhaps be in a better position to take a comprehensive view of which constitution is best, how each must be ordered and what laws and customs it must use if it is to flourish. Very well then, let us make a start.

ST. AUGUSTINE

Confessions of St. Augustine

Chapters 3, 4, 6, 7, 8 and 10

(For groups who wish to do an abridged reading, the
following chapters are recommended: III, IV, VI, VII,
and VIII)

NUMBER 5 | SET TWO

THE GREAT BOOKS FOUNDATION *Chicago*

published and distributed by
THE GREAT BOOKS FOUNDATION
a non-profit educational organization
307 North Michigan Avenue, Chicago, Illinois 60601

CONTENTS

CONTENTS

THE CONFESSIONS OF ST. AUGUSTINE

It's one long prayer

BOOK III

1

I CAME TO Carthage, and all around me in my ears were the sizzling and frying of unholy loves. I was not yet in love, but I loved the idea of love, and from a hidden want I hated myself for not wanting more. Being in love with love I looked for something to love; I hated security and a path without snares. I was starved inside me for inner food (for you yourself, my God), yet this starvation did not make me hungry. I had no desire for the food that is incorruptible, and this was not because I was filled with it; no, the emptier I was, the more my stomach turned against it. And for this reason my soul was in poor health; it burst out into feverish spots which brought the wretched longing to be scratched by contact with the objects of sense. Yet if these had no soul, they could certainly not be loved. It was a sweet thing to me both to love and to be loved, and more sweet still when I was able to enjoy the body of my lover.

And so I muddied the clear spring of friendship with the dirt of physical desire and clouded over its brightness with the dark hell of lust. And still, foul and low as I was, I would, in the exorbitance of my vanity, give myself the airs of a fine man of fashion. Desiring to be captivated in this way, I fell headlong into love. My God and my mercy, how good you were to me in sprinkling so much bitterness over that sweetness! For I was loved myself, and I reached the point where we met together to enjoy our love, and there I was fettered happily in bonds of misery so that I might be beaten with rods of red-hot

1

iron—the rods of jealousy and suspicions, and fears and angers and quarrels.

2

I WAS CARRIED away too by plays on the stage in which I found plenty of examples of my own miseries and plenty of fuel for my own fire. Why is it, I wonder, that people want to feel sad at miserable and tragic happenings which they certainly would not like to suffer themselves? Yet as spectators they do want to suffer the sadness and indeed their whole pleasure is just in this. What a wretched sort of madness! For if one is oneself subject to the kind of emotions one sees on the stage, one is all the more moved by them. Yet when one suffers in real life, this is described as "misery," and when one feels for others, we call it "compassion." But there can be no real compassion for fictions on the stage. A man listening to a play is not called upon to help the sufferer; he is merely invited to feel sad. And the sadder he feels, the higher is his opinion of the actor of this fantasy. If the disasters which happen to people on the stage (disasters which either took place in the remote past or else are pure inventions) are represented in such a way that the spectator does not feel sad, he will go out of the theater in disgust and speak disparagingly of the performance; but so long as he feels sad, he will stay fixed in his place, enjoying every moment.

Are we to say, then, that tears and sufferings are things which we love? Undoubtedly what every man wants is to be glad. Or is it that, while no one wants to be miserable, one still does want to have compassion, and, since one cannot feel compassion without feeling suffering, this and this alone is the reason why sufferings are loved?

This also springs from that vein and source of friendship. But in what direction does it flow? Why is it that it runs into that torrent of pitch which boils and swells with the high tides of foul lust, changing itself into them and of its own will altering its own nature from a heavenly clearness into a precipitation of depravity? Is compassion, then, to be cast out? Certainly not. We must therefore allow ourselves sometimes to love sufferings. But beware of uncleanness, my soul. Stay in the keeping of my God, the *God of our fathers, who is to be praised and exalted above all forever*. Beware of uncleanness.

I have not ceased to feel compassion now. But in those days in the theaters I used to sympathize with the joys of lovers, when they wickedly enjoyed each other, even though all this was purely imaginary and just a stage show, and when they were separated from one another, I used to sympathize with their misery, as though I felt real pity for them; yet I was thoroughly enjoying it in both cases. But now I feel more pity for someone who rejoices in his wickedness than for someone who is supposed to be suffering great hardships because of the lack of some harmful pleasure or the loss of some miserable felicity. This certainly is a truer form of compassion, but the pain in it does not give one pleasure. To feel grief for another's misery is a sign and work of charity and is therefore to be commended; but it is still true that a man who is genuinely compassionate would rather that there was nothing for him to feel grief about. Only if good will could will evil (which is impossible) could there be a man really and truly compassionate who would wish some e to be unhappy so that they could be objects for his compassion. Some sorrow, therefore, may be approved of, but none loved. For this, Lord God, is your way. You are wounded by no sorrow, yet you love souls far more deeply than we can, and your compassion is more lasting and indestructible than ours. *And who is sufficient for these things?*

But I, poor wretch, at that time loved to feel sad and went looking for something to feel sad about; in someone else's sorrow, which was purely fictitious and acted. I was best pleased and most strongly attracted by the performance of an actor who brought tears to my eyes. Unhappy sheep that I was, straying from your flock and impatient of your keeping! No wonder that I became infected with a foul disease, and this was the origin of my love for sorrows—not sorrows that really affected me deeply, for I did not like to suffer in my own person the things which I liked to see represented on the stage, but only those imaginary sorrows the hearing of which had, as it were, the effect of scratching the surface of my skin. And, as happens after the scratching of poisoned nails, what came next were feverish swellings, abscesses, and running sores. Such was the life I led. Was this, my God, a life at all?

3

AND ABOVE ME hovered your mercy, faithful however far I strayed. I wasted myself away in great sins. I followed in the path of sacrilegious curiosity, allowing it to lead me, in my desertion of you, down to the depths of infidelity and the beguiling service of devils, to whom I made my own evil deeds a sacrifice, and in all these things you beat me with your rod. Once when your solemnities were being celebrated within the walls of your Church, I actually dared to desire and then to bring to a conclusion a business which deserved death for its reward. For this you lashed me with punishments that were heavy, but nothing in comparison with my fault, O you infinite mercy, my God, my refuge from those terrible destroyers, among whom I wandered with a stiff neck on my path further and further away from you, loving my own ways and not yours, loving the liberty of a runaway.

Those studies of mine also, which were considered perfectly respectable, were designed to fit me for the law so that I might gain a great name in a profession where those who deceive most people have the biggest reputations. Such is the blindness of men, that blindness should become an actual source of pride! And by now I was a senior student in the School of Rhetoric and very pleased with myself and proud and swelling with arrogance, although, as you know, Lord, I was a quieter character and indeed entirely without any share in the subversive behavior of the "Subverters"—this being the savage and diabolical name which was used as a kind of badge or mark of a "man of the world." However, I kept company with these Subverters and felt a kind of shameless shame for not being like them. I went about with them and there were times when I enjoyed their friendship, though I always hated their actions—that is to say, their "subvertings," which were a kind of wanton persecution of the modesty of ordinary unknown people, a persecution carried out for no reason at all except that by jeering and mocking they were able to give themselves a malicious amusement. Nothing can be more like the behavior of devils than this. "Subverters," therefore, was a very good

name for them. Most clearly they themselves were first
subverted and entirely perverted, and on those occasions
when they took pleasure in mocking and deceiving others,
there were hidden within themselves deceiving spirits,
laughing at them and leading them astray.

4

AMONG SUCH companions in this unsettled age of mine
I pursued my studies of the books of eloquence, a subject
in which I longed to make a name for myself, though
my reason for this was damnable and mere wind, being
simply joy in human vanity. In the normal course of study
I came across a book by Cicero, a man whose style,
though not his heart, is almost universally admired. This
book of his contains an exhortation to philosophy; it is
called *Hortensius*. Now it was this book which altered
my way of feeling, turned my prayers to you, Lord,
yourself, and gave me different ambitions and desires.
Every vain hope suddenly became worthless to me; my
spirit was filled with an extraordinary and burning desire
for the immortality of wisdom, and now I began to rise,
so that I might return to you. I was in my nineteenth
year (my father having died two years previously), and
I might be assumed to be spending the money my mother
sent me on sharpening my tongue; but it was not for the
purpose of sharpening my tongue that I had used this
book of Cicero's; what moved me was not the style, but
the matter.

I was on fire then, my God, I was on fire to leave
earthly things behind and fly back to you, nor did I know
what you would do with me; for with you is wisdom. But
that book inflamed me with the love of wisdom (which
is called "philosophy" in Greek). There are some who

lead us astray by means of philosophy and who use that great and pleasant and honorable name as a disguise or artificial coloring for their own errors, and nearly all such people, both of Cicero's time and before, are noted in that book and censured. There too is clearly stated that wholesome advice given to us by your good and faithful servant: *"Beware lest any man spoil you through philosophy and vain deceit, after the tradition of men, after the rudiments of the world, and not after Christ. For in Him dwelleth all the fullness of the Godhead bodily."* And as to me at that time (you know this, O light of my heart), I was still unacquainted with the Apostolic Scriptures. Yet the one thing in that exhortation which delighted me was this: I was not encouraged by this work of Cicero's to join this or that sect; instead I was urged on and inflamed with a passionate zeal to love and seek and obtain and embrace and hold fast wisdom itself, whatever it might be. And in my ardent desire only one thing held me back, which was that the name of Christ was not there; for this name, Lord, this name of my Saviour, your son, had been with my mother's milk drunk in devoutly by my tender heart, where it remained deeply treasured. So I could not be entirely swept away by anything, however learned or well written or true, which made no mention of this name.

5

I THEREFORE decided to give my attention to the study of the Holy Scriptures and to see what they were like. And what I saw was something that is not discovered by the proud and is not laid open to children; the way in is low and humble, but inside the vault is high and veiled in mysteries, and I lacked the qualities which would make me fit to enter in or stoop my neck to follow the pathway. For when I studied the Scriptures then I did not feel as I am writing about them now. They seemed to me unworthy of comparison with the grand style of Cicero. For my pride shrank from their modesty, and my sharp eye was not penetrating enough to see into their depths. Yet these Scriptures would grow up together with a little child; I, however, thought too highly of myself to become a little child; swollen with pride, I was, in my own eyes, grown-up.

6

AND so I fell in with a sort of people who were arrogant in their madness, too fond of the flesh and too fond of talking, in whose words were the snares of the devil and a kind of birdlime compounded out of a mixture of the syllables of your name and that of the Lord Jesus Christ and of the Holy Ghost, the Comforter. These names were never out of their mouths, but only so far as the sound went and the pronunciation of the words; in their hearts there was no truth whatever. And they kept on saying: "Truth, Truth"; they were forever dinning it in my ears, and *the truth was not in them*. What they said was false, and not only false about you but false about the elements of this world, your creation. And even those philosophers who speak the truth of such things ought to have been disregarded by me for the love of you, my Father and my highest good, O beauty of all things beautiful. O Truth, Truth, how I panted for you even then deep down in the marrow of my soul, when they were constantly and in all kinds of ways making use of the sound of your name— by voice and in their many books and huge tomes. On these dishes there was set before me, in my hunger for

you, the sun and the moon, beautiful creations of yours,
but nevertheless creations of yours and not you yourself,
nor indeed the first of your creations. For your spiritual
creations are before these physical creations, heavenly
and shining as they are. But it was not even for these
first creations of yours that I was hungry and thirsty; it
was for you yourself, Truth, *in whom is no variableness
neither shadow of turning.* But they in those dishes of
theirs kept on putting before me glittering fantasies, and
it would be better to love the actual sun, which is real to
our sight at least, than those false fantasies which make
use of the sight to deceive the mind. Nevertheless, since I
thought that these were you, I fed on them, not with any
great eagerness (for the taste in my mouth was not the
real taste of you, just as you were not these empty fictions), and, so far from being nourished by them, I became the weaker. The food we dream about is very like
the food we see in waking life; yet in our dreams we are
not fed; we are, in fact, asleep. But (as you have since
said to me) those things were not like you in any way;
they were fantasies made out of physical objects, false
objects, since we can place more reliance in those real
objects which we see, whether on earth or in the sky, with
our fleshly sight; animals and birds perceive these objects
just as we do, and they are more real when we see them
than when we imagine them. And again we can have
more confidence in our imagination of them than in
conjectures made from them as to other greater and
infinite objects which in fact do not exist at all.

It was on such things as these that at this time I was fed
—fed without being nourished. But you, my love, for
whom I faint that I may become strong, are not those
objects which we see, though they are in heaven, nor are

you those objects which we do not see there; for all these
things are your creations, and you do not regard them as
among the chief of your creations. How far then are you
from those fantasies of mine, fantasies of objects which do
not exist at all! More real than these are fantasies of objects that do exist, and the objects themselves are still
more real; yet you are not they. Nor are you the soul,
which is the life of bodies, and of course the life of bodies
is better and more real than the bodies themselves. But
you are the life of souls, the life of lives, the very living
life; nor is there change in you, life of my soul. For me,
then, at that time, where were you? How far away? Far
indeed was I straying from you, debarred even from the
husks of the swine whom I fed with husks. For even the
stories of the poets and the masters of literature are better
than these deceitful traps. Verses, poems, and "Medea
flying through the air" are undoubtedly of more use to
one than the Five Elements, variously tricked out to correspond with the Five Dens of Darkness—all of which
have no existence at all and are death to the believer.
For I can turn verses and poems into true nourishment,
and if I declaimed "Medea flying," I was not asserting a
fact, nor, if I heard someone else declaiming the lines, did
I believe them to be true. But those other doctrines I did
believe. And miserably indeed I feel now when I think of
the steps by which I was brought down to the depths of
hell. For want of truth I toiled and I tossed, for I was
seeking for you, my God (this I confess to you who had
pity on me even before I made my confession), not by
means of the intellect and reason (which, according to
your will, set us above the beasts), but by means of the
bodily senses. But you were inside me, deeper than the
deepest recesses of my heart, and you were above me,

higher than the highest I could reach. I had fallen in with
that bold woman in the allegory of Solomon who, *knowing nothing, sits at her door and says: Eat ye bread of
secrecies willingly, and drink ye stolen waters which are
sweet.* She it was who seduced me, for she found my soul
dwelling out of doors, in the eye of my flesh, and chewing
over in myself the cud of what I had eaten through that
eye.

7

FOR I DID NOT know that other reality which truly is,
and it was as though my own sharpness of intelligence
was persuading me to agree with those stupid deceivers
when they put forward their questions: "What is the
origin of evil?" and "Can we imagine a God bounded
by any physical shape and having hair and nails?" and
"Should we consider good those who had many wives at
the same time, who killed men and made animal sacrifices?" In my ignorance I was much disturbed by these
questions, and, as I went further from the truth, I had
the impression that I was drawing nearer to it. This was
because I did not yet know that evil is nothing but a
privation of good, which can continue to the point where
a thing ceases to exist altogether. And how could I see
this, when my eyesight could reach no further than
bodies and the sight of my mind no further than a fantasy?
I did not know that God is a spirit and not one with parts
extended in length and breadth, nor one of whose being
can be used such words as "size," "weight," "bulk." For
everything of that kind must have parts which are less
than the whole, and even if it is infinite there will be less
of it in a part defined by a fixed space than in its total
infinitude, and so it cannot be wholly everywhere, as Spirit

is, as God is. Then too I was ignorant of what in us is the principle of our existence and what is meant by the words of Scripture *"after the image of God"*—as to that I was entirely ignorant.

I was ignorant also of that true and inward goodness which makes its judgments not from convention but from the most right and undeviating law of God Almighty. By this law the customs of different times and places are formed as is right for those times and those places, while the law is the same always and everywhere, not one thing in one place and one in another. According to this Abraham and Isaac and Moses and David and all those men praised by the mouth of God were good men, and to deny that they were good is a mark of ignorance, for it is to judge merely out of man's judgment and to measure the whole moral structure of the human race by one's own particular and partial standard of morality. It is as if someone who knew nothing about armor or what piece of armor was made for each limb were to try to put a shin guard on his head or a helmet on his foot and were then to complain that they fitted badly: or as if, when there was a public holiday in the afternoon, a shopkeeper were to object to not being allowed to keep his shop open then, because he had been allowed to keep it open in the morning; or when in a house one sees one servant handling something or other which the man who carries around the wine would not be allowed to handle; or something done behind the stables which would be forbidden in the dining room; or as if one should be indignant that in one house and one family there is not exactly the same system of distribution to everyone. All this is like the behavior of those who are offended when they hear that good men were allowed to do something in former ages which good men are not allowed to do today; or that, for reasons connected with time, God's commands to those in former times were not the same as his commands are to men of today; yet both in the past and in the present it is the same goodness to which obedience is due. And yet they can see in one man and one day and one household examples of different things being suited to different members, of one thing allowed at one time and not allowed an hour later, or of something permitted or commanded to be done in one corner which is forbidden under pain of punishment to be done in the next corner. Does this mean that justice is something which changes and varies? No, it does not; but the times, over which Justice presides, do not pass by evenly; for they are times. Men however, whose *days are few upon the earth,* cannot by the use of their senses find in previous ages and in other nations of which they have no experience the same relations of cause and effect which they observe in times and peoples of which they have experience. In the case of one body or one day or one house they can easily see what is fitting for each particular member and time and part and person. This argument is convincing, while the more remote argument is often a stumbling block.

At that time I was ignorant of these things and unaware of them. On all sides they were striking me in the eye, but still I did not see them. For instance, when I wrote poetry, I was not allowed to use every kind of foot wherever I liked; different feet had to be used in different meters, and even in the same meter one could not use the same foot in every part of the line. Yet the art of poetry, in accordance with which I wrote, did not have different principles for different occasions; it comprised all the rules together in itself. And I still could not see that the rule of righteousness, followed by these good and holy men, comprised, in a much more lofty and sublime sense, all its precepts together, and that in itself it never varied at all, although at various times, instead of prescribing everything at once, it laid down rules and principles proper for each occasion. So in my blindness I blamed these holy Fathers who not only behaved in their own times as God commanded and inspired them, but also foretold future times as revealed by God.

8

CAN IT at any time or in any place be wrong *to love God with all one's heart, with all one's soul, and with all one's mind; and one's neighbor as oneself?* Therefore, those crimes which are against nature must everywhere and always be detested and punished. The crimes of the men of Sodom are of this kind, and if all nations in the world committed them they would all stand guilty of the same crime against the law of God, which did not design men so that they should use each other in this way. Indeed even that bond which should exist between God and us is violated when the same nature, of which God is the author, is polluted by the perversity of lust. On the other hand in avoiding those actions which are offenses against the customs of men we must take due consideration of the diversity of customs. What has been laid down as a general rule, either by custom or by law, in any city or nation must not be violated simply for the lawless pleasure of anyone, whether citizen or foreigner. For there is faultiness and deficiency in every part that does not fit in with the whole, of which it is a part.

But when God commands that something should be

done which is against the customs or institutions of any people, it must be done, even if it has never been done there before; if it is something that has fallen out of use, then it must be brought back into use, and if it was never a legal obligation, then it must now be made one. We know that it is lawful for a king in the state which he rules over to give an order which has never been given previously either by any of his predecessors or by himself, and that it is not against the general good of the state for him to be obeyed—or rather it would be against the general good if he was not obeyed, since there is a universal agreement in human society that obedience is due to kings. Then how much more unhesitatingly ought we to obey God, the Ruler of all creation, in everything which He commands! For, as in our human societies there are gradations of power, the greater being able to command more obedience than the lesser, so God is set over all.

One may also consider the various cases of sin, when there is a wish to hurt another person, either by insulting him or by injuring him. The motive may be either revenge, as in the case of one enemy against another; or to gain something which belongs to someone else, as with highwaymen against travelers; or to avoid trouble, as when one attacks someone whom one fears; or envy, as when the less fortunate turns against the more fortunate, or when the man who has been successful in something fears the prospect or is angry at the fact of having an equal; or simply the pleasure of seeing others suffer, as in the cases of those who watch gladiators or who mock and make fun of other people. Such sins fall under these headings and they spring from the lust of power, the lust of the eye, the lust of feeling—sometimes from one of these, sometimes from two, sometimes from all three. And so men live badly, against the Three and the Seven, that psaltery of ten strings, your Ten Commandments, O God most high and most sweet. But how can men's insults touch you, who are undefiled? Or what injury can be committed against you, who cannot be hurt? But your vengeance is in that which men do against themselves, because when they sin against you, they are acting wickedly against their own souls, and *iniquity gives itself the lie.* It may be by the corruption or perversion of their own nature, created and ordained by you, or in the immoderate use of things that are allowed, or in the burning lust for things not allowed and for that enjoyment which is against nature; or they may be found guilty of raging against you in their minds and in their words, *kicking against the pricks;* or when they take pleasure in the collapse of the standards of human society and brazenly set up, according to their own likes and dislikes, their private combinations or factions.

And these things are done when you are forsaken O fountain of life, who are the only and the true creator and ruler of the universe, and they proceed from the private and arrogant self-will which falsely attributes unity to a part and loves it. So then the way back to you is through humility and devoutness, and you cleanse us from our evil habits and look mercifully on the sins of those who confess them to you; you hear the groaning of the prisoners and you free us from those fetters which we have made for ourselves—so long as we do not raise against you the standards of an unreal liberty and, in desire for more, risk the loss of everything by setting our love more upon our own private good than upon you, the good of all things.

9

AMONG THE VICES and crimes and the many iniquities that there are must be counted the sins of those who are still making progress. These, if judged aright, will be condemned from the point of view of the rule of perfection, but may be commended if they show hope of future fruit, as is the green blade of the growing corn. And there are some actions which look vicious and criminal and yet are not sins because they are not offenses either against you, our Lord God, or against human society. For example material goods necessary for maintaining life or for some special occasion may be accumulated, and we do not know whether or not the motive was the lust of possession; or, in a zeal for improvement, punishments may be inflicted by the proper authority, but we cannot be sure whether the real motive was or was not a desire to inflict pain. Many actions, therefore, which seem disreputable to men are, according to your testimony, to be approved, and many actions that are praised by men are, in your sight, to be condemned. The appearance of the act, the mind of the person who does the act, and the secret promptings of the occasion are all capable of great variations. But when you suddenly command that something unaccustomed and unforeseen should be done— even if this is something which at one time you forbade, and however much you may hide for the time being the reason for your command and however much it may run contrary to the convention of any particular human society—no one can doubt that this command of yours must be obeyed; since the only just society of men is the society which does your will. But happy are those who recognize your commands! For all the acts of your servants were done either to indicate something which needed showing in their own times, or else to foretell what was to come in the future.

10

I WAS IGNORANT of this, and so I used to mock at those holy servants and prophets of yours. And all my mocking of them meant nothing except that I myself was being mocked by you. Gradually and insensibly I was led on to believe a lot of nonsense, such as that a fig wept when it was picked and that the fig tree, its mother, shed milk-white tears. But if this fig were to be eaten by some Manichaean saint (always assuming that the picking of it was someone else's and not his guilt), it would be digested and then at the end of the process this saint would breathe out from the fig angels, or rather actual particles of God, at every groan or sigh in his prayer, and these particles of the most high and true God would have remained bound up in the fruit if they had not been set free in this way by the mastication and digestion of some sainted "elect." Poor fool that I was, I believed that more mercy ought to be shown to the fruits of the earth than to men, for whom these fruits were created. For supposing some hungry person, not a Manichee, was to ask for a bit and were to be given it, the morsel given would be considered to be as it were condemned to capital punishment.

11

AND YOU stretched out your hand from on high and drew my soul out of that deep darkness. My mother, your faithful servant, was weeping for me to you, weeping more than mothers weep for the bodily deaths of their sons. For she, by that faith and spirit which she had from you, saw the death in which I lay, and you, Lord, heard her prayer. You heard her and you did not despise her tears which fell streaming and watered the ground beneath her eyes in every place where she prayed; indeed you heard her. How otherwise can one explain that dream of hers by which you comforted her and as a result of which she allowed me to live with her and eat at the same table in the house, a thing which she had begun to avoid, since she shrank from and detested the blasphemies of my error? For in her dream she was standing on a sort of wooden ruler, and there came to her a very beautiful young man with a happy face, smiling at her, though she herself was sad and overcome with her sorrow. He then asked her (his purpose being, as is usual in these visions, to instruct her rather than to be instructed) why it was that she was so sad, and she replied that she was weeping for my perdition. Then he told her to have no fear and instructed her to look carefully and see "that where she was, I was too," and when she did look she saw me standing close by her on the same ruler.

Now how could she have dreamed this unless your ears had been open to her heart, O omnipotent Good, you who care for each one of us as though he was your only care and who cares for all of us as though we were all just one person? And how too can this be explained? For when my mother told me her dream, I tried to twist it to a different meaning, namely, that it was she who need not despair of being one day what I was. But she at once and without the slightest hesitation said: "No; for what was told me was not, 'Where he is, you are too.' It was 'Where you are, he is too.'" I confess to you, Lord, that, to the best of my recollection (and I have often spoken of this), I was more moved by this reply given by you through my mother than I was by the dream itself. For my false interpretation was so plausible, yet she was not perplexed by it, and she saw so quickly what was to be seen and what I myself had certainly not perceived before she spoke. So for the consolation of her present distress, joy in the future was promised to this holy woman. And the prediction was made long before the event. For nearly nine years after this I wallowed in the mud of the pit and in the darkness of falsehood, often trying to rise and then being plunged back again all the more violently. Yet all this time that chaste widow, holy and sober (such as you love), though she had now more hope to cheer her, never slackened in her weeping and her lamentations, never ceased in all hours of her prayer to weep to you about me, and her prayers entered into your presence, and yet you still allowed me to roll over and over in that darkness.

12

AND IN THE meantime you gave her another answer, which I remember. For I am leaving out much, since I am hurrying on to those things which I want especially to confess to you, and also there is much that I have forgotten. You did then give her another answer through a priest of yours, a bishop who had been brought up in your Church and was well versed in your books. My mother asked this bishop to be so kind as to discuss things with me, to expose my mistakes, to unteach me what was bad, and to teach me what was good; for he used to do this, if he found suitable people for his instruction. However, he refused to do so in my case, and very sensibly too, as I realized later. He told my mother that I was not yet fit to be taught, because I was full of self-conceit with the novelty of that heresy and had already, as she had told him, been disturbing the minds of people who were not skilled in argument by my captious questions. "But," he said, "let him alone for a while. Only pray to the Lord for him; he himself will find out by his reading what his mistake is and how great is its impiety." And at the same time he told her that he himself, when a small boy, had been handed over to the Manichees by his mother, who had been led astray by them; he had not only read nearly all their books but had actually copied them out, and (with no one to argue with him or attempt to convince him) it had become clear to him that that sect ought to be entirely avoided, and so he had left it. But when he had said this to her, my mother still refused to be satisfied. She kept on begging and praying him, weeping many tears, that he would see me and discuss matters with me. In the end he became somewhat annoyed and said: "Now go away and leave me. As you live, it is impossible that the son of these tears should perish."

And this answer (as she has often mentioned to me in our conversations) she took as though the words had sounded from heaven.

BOOK IV

1

SO FOR THE SPACE of nine years (from my nine-teenth to my twenty-eighth year) I lived a life in which I was seduced and seducing, deceived and deceiving, the prey of various desires. My public life was that of a teacher of what are called "the liberal arts." In private I went under cover of a false kind of religion. I was arrogant in the one sphere, superstitious in the other, and vain and empty from all points of view. On the one hand I and my friends would be hunting after the empty show of popularity—theatrical applause from the audi-ence, verse competitions, contests for crowns of straw, the vanity of the stage, immoderate lusts—and on the other hand we would be trying to get clean of all this filth by carrying food to those people who were called "the elect" and "the holy ones," so that in the factory of their own stomachs they could turn this food into angels and gods, by whose aid we should be liberated. This was my way of life and these were the things I did, I and my friends, who were deceived through me and with me. Let proud-hearted men laugh at me, and those who have not yet, for their own health, been struck down and crushed by you, my God. I shall still confess to you the story of my shame, since it is to your glory. Allow me this, I beg, and grant me the power to survey in my memory now all those wanderings of my error in the past and *to offer unto Thee the sacrifice of rejoicing.* For without you what am I to myself except a guide to my own downfall? Or what am I, even at the best, except an infant sucking the milk you give and feeding upon you, the food that is imperishable? And what sort of a man is any man one can name, seeing that he is only a man? So let the strong and the powerful laugh at us; but let us, weak and needy as we are, make our confession to you.

2

IN THOSE YEARS I taught the art of rhetoric. Overcome myself by a desire for gain, I took money for instructing my pupils how to overcome other people by speechmaking. Nevertheless, Lord, as you know, I preferred to have honest pupils (as honesty is reckoned nowadays); without deceit I taught them the arts of deception, to be used not against the life of any innocent man, though sometimes to save the life of the guilty. And, God, from afar you saw me stumbling in that slippery way and in all that smoke showing just a spark of honor; for in my teaching I did act honorably toward those who loved vanity and sought after a lie, being indeed their companion. In those years I lived with a woman who was not bound to me by lawful marriage; she was one who had come my way because of my wandering desires and my lack of considered judgment; nevertheless, I had only this one woman and I was faithful to her. And with her I learned by my own experience how great a difference there is between the self-restraint of the marriage covenant which is entered into for the sake of having children, and the mere pact made between two people whose love is lustful and who do not want to have children—even though, if children are born, they compel us to love them.

I remember too that once when I had decided to go in for a competition in poetry to be recited on the stage, some magician or other came to me and asked how much

I would give him to be assured of winning the competition, but I loathed and detested the filthy ceremonies of these people, and I told him that, even if the crown to be won were golden and immortal, I would not allow a fly to be killed in order to give me the victory. For his intention was to kill some living creatures in the sacrifices he was going to make and it seemed to me that he meant to try to secure for me the favor of devils by honoring them in this way. Yet in rejecting this evil thing, I was not, O God of my heart, acting out of any pure feeling toward you. I did not know how to love you. I did not know how to think except in terms of a kind of corporeal splendor. And a soul that pants for such figments of the imagination is surely committing fornication against you, is putting its trust in falsity and feeding upon the winds. There was I not allowing this magician to sacrifice to devils on my behalf; yet all the time I was, in that superstition of mind, sacrificing myself to them. For surely to feed them is to feed the winds, and we do this when by our own errors we become objects for their laughter and contempt.

3

THUS I WAS ready enough to consult those imposters called astrologers, my reason being that they made no sacrifices and addressed no prayers to any spirit to assist them in their divinations. Yet true Christian piety must necessarily reject and condemn their art. For *it is a good thing to confess unto Thee,* and to say, *Have mercy upon me, heal my soul, for I have sinned against Thee,* and not to misuse your mercy so as to make it a license for sinning, but to remember the Lord's words: *Behold, thou art made whole, sin no more lest a worse*

thing happen to thee. But the astrologers try to do away
with all this wholesome truth when they say: "The cause
of your sin is inevitably determined by the stars" and
"Venus was responsible here, or Saturn or Mars." As
though man, who is flesh and blood and proud corruption, should be guiltless and the guilt should be laid upon
the creator and the ruler of heaven and of the stars—you,
our God, sweetness and fount of justice, *who shall render
to every man according to his works,* and *a broken and a
contrite heart wilt Thou not despise.*

   The governor of the province at that time was a wise
man who had a great knowledge of medicine and was
very widely known for his skill. He it was who put on
my fevered head the crown which I won in the poetry
contest. But here he was not acting as a doctor for my
fever. That disease can only be cured by you, *who resist
the proud and give grace to the humble.* Nevertheless
you did not fail to help me by means of this old man, nor
did you let slip the opportunity of doing good to my soul.
I grew to know him better and I used to listen eagerly
and intently to what he said. His talk had no great literary
pretensions but was delightful to listen to and also very
much worth hearing because of the liveliness and force
of his opinions. When in the course of conversation he
discovered that I was an eager student of the books of
those who make horoscopes, he spoke to me in a most
kind and fatherly way, urging me to throw away these
books and not to waste on pure nonsense the care and
attention that should be devoted to something useful. He
told me that he himself had in his youth studied astrology
with the idea of adopting it as the profession by which he
would make his living. "And if," he said, "I could understand Hippocrates, there would certainly be no difficulty

in mastering that subject." Nevertheless he had abandoned
astrology and pursued his study of medicine, simply because he had discovered that astrology was a false science,
and, being an honest man, he had no wish to make his
living by deceiving other people. "But you," he said,
"have a profession, the profession of rhetoric, to support
yourself by. You are giving your time to this astrological
nonsense of your own free will and not for any reason of
financial necessity. So you ought to be all the more ready
to believe what I say; for I worked hard to gain a really
thorough knowledge of the subject, with a view to making it my one source of income." I asked him why it was
then that a number of true predictions were made by
astrology, and he, within the limits of his knowledge,
replied that this was due to the force of chance which
was, as it were, distributed through everything in nature.
Often, for instance, while turning over haphazardly the
pages of a book of poetry, one may come upon a line
which is extraordinarily appropriate to some matter which
is in one's own mind, though the poet himself had no
thought of such a thing when he was writing. So, he said,
there was no reason to be surprised if a man's soul, while
quite unconscious of what was going on inside it, should
be acted upon by some higher instinct and should, by
chance and not by any kind of skill, produce an answer
that would fit in well with the affairs or the doings of the
inquirer.

This too, either by him or through him, you did for
me, and it was you who traced in my memory the lines
along which I was later to follow up the inquiry by
myself. But at the time neither he nor my dear friend
Nebridius (a really good and a really pure young man,
who used to laugh at the whole business of divination)

could persuade me to give up these studies. I was still too much impressed by the authority of the astrological writers, and I had not yet found the certain proof that I was looking for, which would make it clear to me beyond all doubt that when these men were consulted and gave a true answer this was by luck or by chance and not from a real science of stargazing.

4

IN THE TIME when I first began to teach rhetoric in the town where I was born, I had found a very dear friend who was following the same studies. We were both of the same age, now at the beginning of manhood; he had grown up with me as a child and we had gone to school together and played together. But he was not in those early days, nor even in this later time, a friend in the true meaning of friendship, because there can be no true friendship unless those who cling to each other are welded together by you in that love which is spread throughout our hearts by the holy spirit which is given to us. But still this friendship was something very sweet to us and had ripened in the enthusiasm of the studies which we had pursued together. For I had turned him away from the true faith (in which, being so young, he was not soundly or thoroughly grounded) and had led him into that deadly superstitious folly of my own, which had so saddened my mother. His mind was wandering astray with mine, and my soul could not be without him. But you were there, you who are always close upon the heels of those who run away from you, you who are at the same time the God of vengeance and the fountain of mercy and who turn us to yourself in ways that are wonderful. You were there, and you took him away from this life, when he had scarcely had a year of this friendship with me, a friendship that was sweeter to me than all sweetnesses that in this life I had ever known.

Who can recount your praises? Who can recount the praises due for what he personally has experienced in himself? What was it, my God, that you did then? And how unsearchable is the abyss of your judgments! For a long time my friend suffered from a high fever and lay unconscious in a sweat that looked like death. When they despaired of his recovery, he was baptized. He knew nothing of this himself, and I paid little attention to the fact of his baptism. I assumed that his soul would retain what it had learned from me and would not be affected by something done to his body while he was unconscious. But it turned out very differently. For he got better and came back to life again, and, as soon as I could speak to him—which was as soon as he could speak to me, since I never left his side and indeed we depended too much on each other—I began to make jokes with him, assuming that he would join in, about the baptism which he had received when he could neither feel nor know what was being done, and yet had now been told that he had received it. But he shrunk back from me as though I were an enemy. With a sudden confident authority which took me aback he told me that, if I wanted to be a friend of his, I must give up talking to him in this way. I was astonished and amazed, and I put off telling him what was in my mind until he should get well again and should be strong enough in health for me to be able to discuss things with him as I wished. But he was taken away beyond the reach of my folly, so that with you he might be kept safe for my comfort. A few days later, when I was not there, his fever returned and he died.

My heart was darkened over with sorrow, and whatever I looked at was death. My own country was a torment to me, my own home was a strange unhappiness. All those things which we had done and said together became, now that he was gone, sheer torture to me. My eyes looked for him everywhere and could not find him. And as to the places where we used to meet I hated all of them for not containing him; nor were they able to say to me now, "Look, he will soon come," as they used to say when he was alive and away from me. I had become a great riddle to myself and I used to ask my soul why it was sad and why it disquieted me so sorely. And my soul did not know what to answer. If I said, "Trust in God," she very rightly did not obey me, because the man whom she had lost, my dearest friend, was more real and better than the fantastic god in whom she was asked to trust. Only tears were sweet to me, and tears had taken the place of my friend in my heart's love.

5

AND NOW, LORD, all that has passed and time has dulled my pain. May I learn from you, who are Truth, and may I put close to your mouth the ear of my heart so that you can tell me why it is that tears are sweet to us when we are unhappy? Or have you, in spite of the fact that you are present everywhere, put our unhappiness far from you? You abide in yourself, while we are tossed about from one trial to another. And yet if we could not speak our misery into your ears, there would be nothing at all left to us of hope. How is it, then, that from the bitterness of life we can pluck such sweet fruit in mourning and weeping and sighing and lamentation? Is the sweetness simply in the fact that we hope that you are listening to us? This is certainly so in the case of our prayers, since our prayers have a longing to reach you. But is it also so in the case of that sorrow and grief felt for something lost, in which I was overwhelmed at that time? For I had no hope that he would come back to life again, and this was not what I begged for with my tears; I merely felt sad and I wept; for I was in misery and I had lost my joy. Or is weeping really a bitter thing, and is it only pleasant to us at the moment when we are shrinking back from the things we once enjoyed and can scarcely bear to think of them?

6

BUT WHY am I saying all this? It is not the time now to be asking questions but for making my confession to you. I was unhappy and so is every soul unhappy which is tied to its love for mortal things; when it loses them, it is torn in pieces, and it is then that it comes to realize the unhappiness which was there even before it lost them. Such was I at that time, and I wept most bitterly, and I found repose in bitterness. Indeed I was unhappy, yet this unhappy life of mine was dearer to me than the friend whom I had lost. Certainly I would have liked to change my life, but not to part with it; I would prefer rather to part with my friend. And I doubt whether I would have parted with it even for his sake—as in the story, or fable, of Orestes and Pylades, who both wanted to die together, each for each, at the same time, since not to live together was worse to them than death. But I had a strange kind of feeling, which was just the opposite of theirs: I was at the same time thoroughly tired of living and extremely frightened of dying. The fact was, I think, that the more I loved my friend, the more I hated and feared death which, like a cruel enemy, had taken him away from me, and I imagined that, since it had been able to destroy him, it would quickly and suddenly destroy all men living. Yes; I remember it well; this was how I thought. Look, my God, into my heart; look inside it; see, because I remember, O my hope, you who cleanse me from the uncleanness of such affections, directing *mine eyes toward Thee and plucking my feet out of the snare.* I was surprised that other mortals could remain alive when the man, whom I had loved as though he would never die, was dead. And I was still more surprised that, when he was dead, I, who was his other self, should still live. I agree with the poet who called his friend "the half of his own soul." For I felt that my soul and my friend's had been one soul in two bodies, and that was why I had a horror of living, because I did not want to live as a half being, and perhaps too that was why I feared to die, because I did not want him, whom I had loved so much, to die wholly and completely.

7

WHAT MADNESS it is not to know how to love men as they should be loved! And how foolish man is to be violent and impatient with the lot of man. Mad and foolish I was at that time. I raged and sighed and wept and worried, I could not rest, I could not think intelligently. For I was carrying about with me my soul all broken and bleeding and not wanting to be carried by me; yet I did not know where to put it down. There was no rest for it anywhere—not in pleasant groves, not in games and singing, not in sweet-smelling gardens, not in fine banquets, not in the pleasures of the bed, not in the reading of books, nor in poetry. I loathed everything, even the light itself, and everything that was not he seemed to me painful and wearisome, except for my tears and my laments; for in these alone I did find a little peace. But as soon as my soul was distracted from weeping, I became overwhelmed by a great load of unhappiness. It was a load which I should have brought to you, Lord, for you to lighten. I knew this but I neither would nor could—all the more so because, when I thought of you, I was not thinking of something firm and solid. For it was not you yourself who were my God; my god was an empty fantasy, a creation of my own error. If I tried to lay down my burden there, that it might rest, it slipped through the void and came tumbling back upon me again. And myself to myself had become a place of misery, a place where I could not bear to be and from which I could not go. For my heart could not flee away from my heart, nor could I escape from myself, since wherever I ran, I should be following. Nevertheless I did flee from my native place; for my eyes did not search for him so much in places where they were not accustomed to see him. So I left the town of Tagaste and came to Carthage.

8

TIME IS NOT inactive. So far from passing through our senses without doing anything, it performs wonders in our minds. So now time came and went from one day to another, and in its coming and going it gave me other things to hope for and other things to remember, and gradually patched me up again with the sort of pleasures which I had known before. To these pleasures my great sorrow began to give way. But, though its place was not taken by other sorrows, it was taken by things which could cause other sorrows. For the reason why that great sorrow of mine had pierced into me so easily and so deeply was simply this: I had poured out my soul like water onto sand by loving a man who was bound to die just as if he were an immortal. Now certainly what did me most good and helped most to cure me was the comfort I found in other friends, in whose company I loved all the things which, after this, I did love. And this was one huge fable, one long lie; by its adulterous caressing, my mind, which lay itching in my ears, was corrupted. Nor, if one of my friends died, would that fable die out in me. There were other things which more fully took up my mind in their company—to talk and laugh and do kindnesses to each other; to read pleasant books together; to make jokes together and then talk seriously together; sometimes to disagree, but without any ill feeling, just as one may disagree with oneself, and to find that these very rare disagreements made our general agreement all the sweeter; to be sometimes teaching and sometimes learning; to long impatiently for the absent and to welcome them with joy when they returned to us. These and other similar expressions of feeling, which proceed from the hearts of those who love and are loved in return, and are revealed in the face, the voice, the eyes, and in a thousand charming ways, were like a kindling fire to melt our souls together and out of many to make us one.

9

IT IS THIS which we love in our friends, and we love it so much that a man's conscience will condemn him if he fails to give or accept friendship when it is sought for or offered; nor will he expect anything else of a physical nature from his friend except these demonstrations of good feeling. It is for this that we feel such sorrow if a friend dies, such darkness of pain, the heart steeped in tears, all sweetness turned to bitterness, and for us a kind of living death because we have lost in death one who was alive. Blessed is the man who loves you, who loves his friend in you, and his enemy because of you. He alone loses no one dear to him, for they are all dear to him in one who is not lost. And who is this except our God, the God who made heaven and earth and who fills them, because it was by filling them that He created them? No one loses you, except one who voluntarily leaves you. And if he leaves you, where can he go, or where can he escape from you? He can only run from your kindness to your anger. Everywhere in his own punishment he will encounter your law. And your law is truth, and truth is you.

10

Turn us, O God of hosts, show us thy countenance and we shall be whole. For wherever man's soul turns, except toward you, it is fixed to sorrows, even if it fixes itself on things of beauty outside you and outside itself. These things of beauty would have no existence at all unless they were from you. They rise and set; in their rising they begin, as it were, to exist; they develop so as to reach their perfection, and after that they grow old and die; not all grow old, but all die. So, when they rise and reach their way into existence, the quicker they are to grow into being, the more they hurry toward ceasing to be. That is their law. So much you have given them, namely to be parts of a structure in which the parts are not all in existence at the same time; instead, by fading and by replacing each other, they all together constitute the universe of which they are parts. Our own speech too, which is constructed out of meaningful sounds, follows the same principles. There could never be a complete sentence unless one word, as soon as the syllables had been sounded, ceased to be in order to make room for the next. In these things let my soul praise you, God, creator of all things, yet let it not be stuck and glued too close to them in love through the senses of the body. For these things go along their path toward nonexistence, and they tear and wound the soul with terrible longings, since the soul itself desires to be and to find rest in what it loves. But in those things there is no place to rest, since they do not stay. They pass away and no one can follow them with his bodily senses. Nor can anyone grasp them tight even while they are present and in front of him.

Our bodily sense is slow because it is bodily sense and is bounded by the physical. It is sufficient for the purpose for which it was made, but it is quite incapable of grasping and holding things as they run on their appointed way from their beginnings to their endings. For in your word, by which they are created, they hear their decree: "From this point; and not beyond that."

11

DO NOT BE FOOLISH, my soul, and do not let the ear of your heart be deafened by the din of your folly. Listen now. The Word itself calls you to come back; and there is the place of peace that is imperturbable, where love cannot be forsaken unless it first forsakes. See how things pass away so that other things may take their places and that so this lower universe may be established in all its parts. "But do I ever depart," says the Word of God, "and is there any place to which I could depart?" There fix your dwelling place, my soul, and there store up everything which you have received from there. Do it now at least, tired out as you are with falsities. Entrust to truth whatever truth has given you, and you will lose nothing. What is withered in you will flower again, and all your illnesses will be made well, and all that was flowing and wasting from you will regain shape and substance and will form part of you again, and they will not lay you down in the place where they themselves descend, but will stand fast with you and abide with you forever before God who stands and abides forever.

Why then be perverse, my soul, and why follow your own flesh? Will you not rather turn and let your flesh follow you? Whatever you perceive through the flesh you perceive only in part, and you are ignorant of the whole, of which these are parts; yet still these parts delight you. But if your bodily sense were capable of comprehending the whole—instead of being, for your punishment, justly restricted itself to a part of the universe—you would wish that everything in existence at the present moment would pass and go, so that you might have the greater pleasure of perceiving the entirety of things. For these words we speak are perceived by you through your bodily sense, and you certainly do not want to hear the same syllables forever; you want them to pass away so that others may come and so that you may hear the whole sentence. And this is always the case when one thing is made up of many parts and all the parts do not exist together at the same time. To perceive all the parts together at once would give more pleasure than to perceive each individual part separately. But far better than these is He who made all things, and He is our God.

And He does not pass away, because there is nothing to take His place.

12

IF BODIES PLEASE YOU, praise God for them and turn your love back from them to their maker, lest you should displease Him in being pleased by them. If souls please you, love them in God, because by themselves they are subject to change, but in Him they are established firm; without Him they would pass away and be no more. So you must love them in Him and take with you to Him as many souls as you can and say to them: "It is He whom we must love; He made all this and He is not far off." For He did not make things and then go away; things are from Him and also in Him. See where He is: He is everywhere where there is the least trace of truth. He is right inside the heart, but the heart has wandered away from Him. Return, sinners, to your own heart and cling to Him who made you. Stand in Him, and you shall stand fast; rest in Him, and you shall find peace. Where are you going to over those rough paths? Where are you going? The good that you love is from Him; but its goodness and sweetness is only because you are looking toward Him; it will rightly turn to bitterness if what is from Him is wrongly loved, He Himself being left out of the account. What are you aiming at, then, by going on and on walking along these difficult and tiring ways? There is no rest to be found where you are looking for it. Seek what you seek, but it is not there where you are seeking. You seek a happy life in the country of death. It is not there. For how can life be happy, where there is no life?

But our Life came down to us and suffered our death

and destroyed death by the abundance of His own life: and He thundered, calling us to return to Him into that secret place from which He came out to us—coming first into the Virgin's womb, where humanity was married to Him, our mortal flesh, that it might not be forever mortal, and from there *like a bridegroom coming out of His chamber, rejoicing as a giant to run His course.* For He was not slow; He ran, crying aloud in His words, in His deeds, in His death, in His life, in His descent, in His ascension, crying and calling us to return to Him. And He withdrew Himself from our eyes so that we might return to our heart and find Him. He went away, and, look, He is here. He did not want to be with us long, and He has not left us. He went back to a place which He had never left, since the world was made by Him and He was in this world, and He came into this world to save sinners. It is to Him that my soul makes confession, and He heals my soul, for it has sinned against Him. Sons of men, how long will you be so slow and heavy of heart? Now that Life has come down to you, will you not raise yourselves and live? But how can you raise yourselves, when you are already high in the air and have *set your mouth against the heavens?* Come down, so that you may go up and go up toward God. For in climbing up against God, you fell. Say this to the souls you love. Tell them to weep in this valley of tears, and so carry them up with you to God, because it is by His spirit that you are saying this to them, if, while you say it, you are burning with the fire of charity.

13

AT THAT TIME I did not know this and I loved these lower beauties and I was sinking down to the depths.

I used to say to my friends, "Do we love anything except what is beautiful? What, then, is the beautiful? And what is beauty? What is it that attracts us and wins our affection for the things we love? For unless there were grace and beauty in them, they could not possibly draw us to them." And, observing things closely, I saw that in bodies themselves there was one sort of beauty which comes from a thing constituting a whole, and another sort of grace which comes from the right and apt relationship of one thing to another, such as one part of a body to the whole body, or a shoe to the foot, and so on. This idea sprang up into my mind from the depths of my heart, and I wrote some books on "The Beautiful and the Fitting"—two or three books, I think. You know, God, for I cannot remember. I no longer have the books. Somehow or other they have disappeared.

14

WHY WAS IT, LORD my God, that I decided to dedicate these books to Hiereus, who was an orator at Rome? I had never seen the man, but I had come to love him because of his very great reputation for learning, and I had heard and very much admired some of the things he had said. But the greater part of my admiration came from the fact that others admired him. He was praised to the skies and people were astonished that he, a Syrian who was brought up as a master of Greek oratory, should later become such a wonderful speaker in Latin and should also possess such a wide knowledge of philosophy. So he was praised and, without ever having been seen, was loved. Does this kind of love come into the heart of the hearer straight from the words of praise which he hears? Not at all. What happens is that love is kindled by love. We only

40 40 The Confessions of St. Augustine

40 love someone whom we hear praised when we believe that the praise comes from a sincere heart, that is to say, when the man who gives the praise loves the man whom he is praising.

So at that time I loved men on the strength of the judgment of other men—not on your judgment, my God, in whom no one is deceived. Yet my feeling was not like that which one may have for a famous charioteer or a fighter with wild beasts in the theater who is the idol of the crowd. My feelings were different and more serious, and I admired others as I would have liked to be admired myself. For I would not have wanted to be praised and loved as actors are, though I myself would certainly praise and love actors. But I would rather have been quite unknown than known in that way, rather have been hated than loved like that. How does it come about that the weights and impulses toward all these different kinds of love are distributed in one soul? Why is it that I love some quality in another man and yet would appear to hate it too, since I should reject it and detest it in myself? We are both of us human; the actor and I share the same nature, so one cannot compare my feeling about him with the feeling of a man who loves a good horse but would not like to be a horse, even if he could. How is it then that I love in a human being something which I should hate in myself, though I also am a human being? Man himself is a great deep, and you, Lord, number the very hairs of his head and in your sight they are not lost. Yet the hairs of man's head are easier to number than are his affections and the impulses of his heart.

That orator, however, whom I loved so much, was the kind of man that I would have wished to be myself. And I erred through swelling pride; I was tossed about by

every wind, and it was too difficult for me to feel your
steering hand. Why is it that I know now, and can confess it to you confidently, that I loved that man more
because of the love of those who praised him than because of the actual qualities for which he was praised?
The fact is that if the same people, instead of praising him,
had abused him and had said just the same things about
him in an abusive and contemptuous spirit, I should not
have been so set on fire with admiration for him; yet his
qualities would have been just the same; the man himself
would have been no different; the only differences would
have been in the feelings of the speakers. See how abject
and helpless the soul is before it learns to cling to the
solidity of truth! As the winds of speech blow from the
hearts of those who hold their varying opinions, so the
soul is carried this way and that, changing its course now
here, now there; its light is clouded over, and it cannot see
the truth. And there is the truth, right in front of us. And
to me it was a matter of great importance for my style
and my work to become known to that famous orator,
and if he liked them, I should be all the more ardent
about him; though if he thought little of them, then my
vain heart, quite empty of your solidity, would be
wounded. Yet still I enjoyed my meditations on "The
Beautiful and the Fitting," which I dedicated to him,
and, if there was no one else to admire the work, I
thought it very good myself.

15

BUT, ALMIGHTY, I did not yet see that all this great
matter has its hinge in your workmanship; for you alone
make wonders, and my mind was ranging over corporeal
forms. I defined and distinguished the beautiful as being

that which is beautiful in itself and the fitting as being that which derives its grace from its appropriateness to something else, and I used corporeal examples in support of my argument. I also considered the nature of the mind, but the false view I had of spiritual things prevented me from seeing the truth. And the very force of truth itself was staring me in the face, but I turned my panting mind away from what was incorporeal and concentrated on line and color and swelling magnitudes, and because I could not see these in my mind, I concluded that I could not see my mind. And as in virtue I loved peace and in vice I hated discord, so I noted the unity in the one and the division, as it were, in the other, and it seemed to me that in the unity lay the rational mind and the nature of truth and the supreme good; but in the division I was wretched enough to imagine that I saw some sort of substance of the irrational life and a nature of the supreme evil, which was not only substance but actually life—yet not proceeding from you, my God, from whom proceed all things. I called the first a Monad, conceiving of it as a mind without any sex, and I called the other a Dyad—anger as in deeds of violence, and lust as in sins of impurity. I was talking ignorantly. I did not know and I had not yet been taught that evil is not a substance at all nor is our soul that supreme and unchangeable good.

For just as acts of violence are done if the emotion, in which lies the impulse to act, is vicious and aggressive and muddled, and just as sins of impurity are done if the affection of the soul from which carnal pleasures are derived is uncontrolled, so errors and false opinions contaminate life if the rational soul itself is corrupted. And so it was with me at that time, when I did not know that my soul needed to be illumined by another light, if it was to be a partaker of truth, since it is not itself the essence of truth. *For Thou shalt light my candle, O Lord my God, Thou shalt enlighten my darkness:* and *of Thy fullness have we all received, for Thou art the true light that lighteth every man that cometh into the world; for in Thee there is no variableness, neither shadow of change.*

But I was aiming to reach you and at the same time was being forced back from you, so that I might taste death; for *Thou resistest the proud.* And how could anything be more proud than to assert, as I did in my incredible folly, that I was by nature what you are? For, being subject to change myself (as was obvious from the mere fact that I wanted to become wise and so proceed from worse to better), I preferred to think that you also were subject to change rather than I was not what you are. And so I was forced back from you and you resisted my vain stiff-neckedness, and I imagined corporeal forms, and, being myself flesh, I accused the flesh, and, being a wayfaring spirit, I did not return to you, but went on and on wandering into fancies which have no existence either in you or in me or in the body and, so far from being created for me by your truth, were figments constructed by my imagination out of corporeal things. And I used to speak to the little ones of your faith—my own fellow citizens, though I, without knowing it, was in exile from them—and, like a talkative ass, I used to say, "How is it, then, that the soul makes a mistake if it was created by God?" But I would not allow myself to be asked, "How is it, then, that God makes a mistake?" And I preferred to maintain that your unchangeable substance went astray under compulsion, rather than admit that my own changeable substance had deviated of its own accord and for its punishment had fallen into error.

I was about twenty-six or twenty-seven when I wrote

those books. As I wrote them I turned over in my mind all those corporeal fictions which made such a noise that the ears of my heart were deafened. Yet, sweet truth, I was straining these ears to try to hear your inner melody, as I meditated upon "The Beautiful and the Fitting"; and I longed to stand and hear you and rejoice with joy at the voice of the bridegroom; but I could not. I was being dragged out and away by the voices of my own error, and I was sinking down to the depths under the weight of my own pride. You did not *make me to hear joy and gladness* nor did *the bones exult which were not yet humbled.*

16

AND WHAT GOOD did it do me that at about the age of twenty I was able to read and understand without any help that book of Aristotle's called *The Ten Categories* when it came into my hands? My rhetoric master at Carthage and others too with a reputation for learning would puff out their cheeks with pride whenever they mentioned this book, and so I was looking forward to it eagerly as though it was something wonderful and inspired. Later I compared notes with people who told me that they had had the greatest difficulty in understanding this book, even with the help of most learned commentators who had explained matters not only in words but by diagrams drawn in the sand. However they could tell me no more about the book than what I had discovered by reading it myself. Indeed the book seemed to me to deal very clearly with substances, such as "man," and with their qualities, such as the figure of a man; what sort of man he is; his height, how many feet; his family relationships, whose brother he is; where he is placed;

when he was born; whether he is standing or sitting; whether he is wearing shoes or armor; whether he is doing something or having something done to him—and all the other innumerable things that can be put either in these nine categories of which I have given examples, or else in the main category of substance.

All this, so far from doing me any good, actually did me harm. For, imagining that everything in existence could be placed under these ten categories, I attempted by this method to understand you, my God, in your wonderful simplicity and changelessness, as though you were a substance with the qualities of your own greatness or your own beauty, as we find qualities in a body. But you yourself are your greatness and your beauty, but a body is not great or beautiful simply by the fact of being a body, since it would still be a body if it were less great or less beautiful. My thoughts of you were falsehood and not truth, fictions of my misery and not the realities of your blessedness. You gave the order, and so it was done in me, that the *earth should bring forth briars and thorns to me* and that *in the sweat of my brows I should eat my bread*.

And what good did it do me that I, at a time when I was the vile slave of evil desires, read and understood for myself every book that I could lay my hands on which dealt with what are called the liberal arts? I enjoyed these books and did not know the source of whatever in them was true and certain. For I had my back to the light and my face to the things on which the light shone; so the eyes in my face saw things in the light, but on my face itself no light fell. I could understand quite easily and without the aid of an instructor every work on rhetoric or logic, geometry, music, and arithmetic. This you know, my Lord God, since quickness of intelligence and precision in understanding are your gifts. But I did not use these gifts by making an offering of them to you. And so it all turned more to my destruction than to my profit, because I labored to secure so good a portion of my substance in my own power, and, instead of preserving my strength for you, I went away from you into a far country to waste my substance upon false and prostitute desires. For what good could my good abilities do me if I did not use them well? I never realized that even hardworking and talented people find these arts very difficult to understand until I began to try to explain them to others; then I found that the real experts in them were the ones who could follow my explanations reasonably quickly.

But what good was all this to me, holding, as I did, that you, Lord God and Truth, were a vast luminous body and that I was a sort of piece broken off from this body? What an extraordinary perversity I showed! Yet this was what I was then. And now, my God, I do not blush to confess to you the mercies which you have shown me and to call upon you—I who did not blush then, when I was professing my blasphemies before men and raising my barking voice against you. What good to me then was that intelligence of mine, so quick and nimble in those arts and sciences? What good to me were all those knotty volumes which I unraveled without the aid of any human teacher, when all the time I was so disgracefully, so sacrilegiously, and so foully wrong in the doctrine of piety? Or what great harm was it to your little ones, if they had a far slower intelligence than mine, since they did not go far from you, and so were able safely to become fledged in the nest of your Church and nourish the wings of charity on the food of a sound faith?

O Lord our God, *under the shadow of Thy wings let us hope.* Protect us and bear us up. You will bear us up, yes, from our infancy until our gray hairs you will bear us up. For our strength, when it is from you, is strength indeed; but when it is our own, it is weakness. With you our good is ever living, and when we turn our backs on it, then we are perverse. Let us return now to you, Lord, so that we may not be overturned, because our good is with you, living and without any defect, since you yourself are our good. And we need not be afraid of having no place to which we may return. We of our own accord fell from that place. And our home, which is your eternity, does not fall down when we are away from it.

BOOK VI

1

HOPE OF MINE from my youth, where were you and where had you gone from me? Was it not you who had created me and distinguished me from the beasts of the field and made me wiser than the birds of the air? Yet I walked through shadows and on slippery ways, and I searched for you outside me and did not find the God of my heart. I had come to the depths of the sea, and I had no confidence or hope of discovering the truth.

By this time my mother had joined me. Her piety had given her strength and she had followed me over land and sea, confident in you throughout all dangers. In the perils of the sea it was she who put fresh heart into the sailors although as a rule it is for the sailors to reassure the passengers who are inexperienced on the high seas. But she promised them that they would get safely to land because you had promised this to her in a vision. She found me in grave danger indeed, my danger being that of despairing of ever discovering the truth. I told her that, though I was not yet a Catholic Christian, I was certainly no longer a Manichaean; but she showed no great signs of delight, as though at some unexpected piece of news, because she already felt at ease regarding that particular aspect of my misery; she bewailed me as one dead, certainly, but as one who would be raised up again by you; she was in her mind laying me before you on the bier so that you might say to the widow's son: *"Young man, I say unto thee, Arise,"* and he should revive and begin to speak and you should give him to his mother. So her heart was shaken by no storm of exultation when she

48

heard that what she had daily begged you with her tears should happen had in so large a part taken place—that I was now rescued from falsehood, even though I had not yet attained the truth. She was indeed quite certain that you, who had promised her the whole, would give her the part that remained, and she replied to me very calmly and with a heart full of confidence that she believed in Christ that, before she departed from this life, she would see me a true Catholic. So much she said to me. But to you, fountain of mercies, she poured out her prayers and her tears more copiously than before, begging you to hasten your help and to lighten my darkness, and she would hurry more eagerly than ever to church and hang upon the words of Ambrose, praying for *the fountain of that water, which springeth up into life everlasting.* For she loved that man as though he were an angel of God, because she knew that it was through him that I had been brought for the time being to this doubtful wavering state of mind, and she was perfectly certain that I would pass through this from sickness to health, though before then I should be exposed to a more serious attack, like that which doctors call "the crisis."

2

THERE WAS an occasion when my mother had brought, as was her custom in Africa, cakes and bread and wine to some of the chapels built in memory of the saints and was forbidden to do this by the doorkeeper. When she found that it was the bishop who had forbidden this practice, she accepted his ban so devoutly and so willingly that I myself was amazed to see how much more readily now she would condemn her own practice of the past than dispute the bishop's prohibition. For her soul was not a victim to the craving for wine, and no liking for wine stimulated her into a hatred for the truth—a thing which happens to many people of both sexes who are just as disgusted by a hymn of sobriety as real drunkards are if their wine is mixed with water. But when my mother brought her basket with the usual sorts of food, which were first to be tasted by her and then given away, she never took more than one small cup well watered down to suit her sober taste, and this was just for the sake of courtesy. And if there were many memorial chapels which she thought ought to be honored in this way, she still carried this same cup around with her to be used at each place; in the end it would be not only nearly all water, but also lukewarm, and she would share this out in small sips with those around her; for she came then to look for piety, not for pleasure. But when she found that that famous preacher and that great example of piety had forbidden the practice even to those who used it soberly—so that drunkards should not be given an occasion for excess and also because this kind of anniversary funeral feast is very much like the superstitious ceremony of the pagans—she most willingly gave up her old habit. Instead of a basket filled with the fruits of the earth, she had learned to bring to the chapels of the Martyrs a breast full of something much purer, her prayers. So she was able to give what she could spare to the poor, and so the communion of the Lord's body might be celebrated in those places where, in imitation of His passion, the martyrs had lost their lives and won their crowns.

And yet it seems to me, my Lord God—and on this matter my heart lies open in your sight—that in abandoning this old custom of hers my mother might possibly not have given way so easily if the prohibition had come from someone else whom she did not love as she loved Ambrose. For she loved him very greatly on account of my salvation, and he loved her for her religious way of life; for she was always doing good works, was fervent in spirit, and constantly at church. So that when he saw me he often used to burst forth in her praises, congratulating me on having such a mother, though he was unaware of what sort of a son she had in me—one who was in doubt on all these matters and who thought that there was no possibility of finding the way of life.

3

I WAS NOT YET groaning in prayer for you to help me. My mind was intent on inquiry and restless in dispute. I considered Ambrose himself, who was honored by people of such importance, a lucky man by worldly standards; only his celibacy seemed to me rather a burden to bear. But I could neither guess nor tell from my own experience what hope he had within him, what were his struggles against the temptations of his exalted position, what solace he found in adversity; nor could I tell of that hidden mouth of his (the mouth of his heart), what joys it tasted in the rumination of your bread. And he on his side did not know of the turmoil in which I was or the deep pit of danger before my feet. I was not able to ask him the questions I wanted to ask in the way I wanted to ask them, because I was prevented from having an intimate conversation with him by the crowds of people, all of whom had some business with him and to whose infirmities he was a servant. And for the very short periods of time when he was not with them, he was either refreshing his body with necessary food or his mind with reading. When he was reading, his eyes went over the pages and his heart looked into the sense, but voice and tongue were resting. Often when we came to him (for no one was forbidden to come in, and it was not customary for visitors even to be announced) we found him reading, always to himself and never otherwise; we would sit in silence for a long time, not venturing to interrupt him in his intense concentration on his task, and then we would go away again. We guessed that in the very small time which he was able to set aside for mental refreshment he wanted to be free from the disturbance of other people's business and would not like to have his attention distracted; also we thought that he might be taking precautions in case, if he read aloud in the presence of some eager and interested person, he might have to give a lecture on the obscure points in the author whom he was reading, or enter into a discussion on the questions of difficulty, with the result that, after he had spent time on this, he would not be able to read as many books as he wanted to read. Though perhaps a more likely reason for his reading to himself was that he wanted to preserve his voice, which grew tired very easily. But whatever his reason was for acting in this way it would certainly be a good one.

Anyhow, I was given no chance of making the inquiries I wished to make from that holy oracle of yours, his breast. I could only ask things that would not take long in the hearing. But I needed to find him with plenty of time to spare if I was to pour out to him the full flood of agitation boiling up inside me, and I could never find him like this. Yet every Sunday I listened to him rightly preaching to the people the word of truth, and I became more and more sure that all those knots of cunning calumny which, in their attacks on the holy books, my deceivers had tied could be unraveled. In particular I discovered that the phrase "man, created by Thee, after Thine own image" was not understood by your spiritual children, whom you have made to be born again by grace through the Catholic mother, in such a way as to mean that you are bounded by the shape of a human body. And although I had not the faintest or most shadowy notion about what a spiritual substance could be, nevertheless with a kind of pleasant shame I blushed to think of how for all these years I had been barking not against the Catholic faith but against figments of carnal imaginations. And indeed I had been rash and impious; for I had spoken in condemnation of things which I ought to have taken the trouble to find out about. But you, the highest, and the nearest, most hidden and most present, have no limbs or parts greater and smaller; you are everywhere in your entirety, yet limited by no particular space; you are not of any bodily form, yet you made man "after your own image" and, see, man is in space from head to foot.

4

BEING IGNORANT, then, of how this image of yours could subsist, I ought to have knocked at the door and asked in what sense the doctrine was to be believed, instead of insulting and attacking what I assumed to be the accepted doctrine. And so my anxiety as to what I could hold for certain gnawed at my inmost heart all the more keenly as I felt the more ashamed of myself for having been so long deluded and deceived by the promise of certainties and then having, with a quite childish inaccuracy and enthusiasm, gone on and on proclaiming uncertainties as though they were truths. That they were actual falsehoods only became clear to me later. What was certain was that they were uncertain and that I for some time had accepted them as certainties when, in my blind zeal for contention, I was attacking your Catholic Church. I had not yet discovered that this Church was teaching the truth, but at least I now knew that it was not teaching the things which I had so vigorously attacked. So I was both confounded and converted, and I was glad, my God, that your only Church, the body of your only son—that Church in which the name of Christ had been put upon me as an infant—was not flavored with this childish nonsense and did not, in her healthy doctrine, maintain the view that you, the Creator of all things, could be, in the form of a human body, packed into a definite space which, however mighty and large, must still be bounded on all sides.

I was glad too that the old Scriptures of the Law and the Prophets were set before me in such a way that I could now read in a different spirit from that which I had had before, when I used to criticize your holy ones for holding various views which, plainly, they never held at all. And I was happy when I heard Ambrose in his sermons, as I often did, recommend most emphatically to his congregation this text as a rule to go by: *The letter killeth, but the spirit giveth life.* So he would draw aside the veil of mystery and explain in a spiritual sense the meanings of things which, if understood literally, appeared to be teaching what was wrong. And I could raise no objections to what he said, even though I was still not sure whether what he said was true or not. I held my heart back from positively accepting anything, since I was afraid of another fall, and in this condition of suspense I was being all the more killed. I wanted to be just as certain about things which I could not see as I was

certain that seven and three make ten. For I was not quite
mad enough as to think that even this proposition is
beyond our comprehension; but I did demand the same
degree of certainty with regard to other things, whether
they were material things not present to my senses or
spiritual things, of which I could form no conception except in material terms. By believing I might have been
cured, so that the sight of my mind would be clearer and
might be somehow or other directed toward your truth
which is the same forever and in no point fails. But it was
the same with me as with a man who, having once had a
bad doctor, is afraid of trusting himself even to a good
one. So it was with the health of my soul which could
not possibly be cured except by believing, but refused to
be cured for fear of believing something falser. So I resisted your hands, for it was you who prepared the medi-
cines of faith and applied them to the diseases of the
world and gave them such potency.

5

FROM NOW ON, however, I began to prefer the Catholic
faith. In requiring belief in what was not demonstrated
(and this includes both things that cannot be proved
at all and things which, though capable of being proved,
cannot be proved to everyone) I felt that the Catholic
faith showed more modesty and more honesty than did
the Manichees, who made rash promises of certain
knowledge, derided credulity, and then produced a lot of
fabulous absurdities in which we were required to believe
because they were not susceptible of proof. Finally it
was you, Lord, who with your most tender and merciful
hand gradually laid hold upon my heart and settled it
in calm. I considered what a countless number of things

there were which I believed though I had not seen them and had not been present when they had taken place— so many historical events, so many facts about countries and cities which I had never seen, so many things told me by friends, by doctors, by one man or another man— and unless we believed these things, we should get nothing done at all in this life. Then in particular I considered how fixed and unalterable was the belief I held that I was the son of a particular father and mother, a thing which I could not possibly know unless I had believed it on the word of others. And so by these considerations you led me to see that the people to be blamed were not those who believed in those books of yours, which you have established with such authority in nearly every nation of the world, but those who did not believe in them, and that I ought not to pay any attention to anyone who might say to me: "How do you know that those books were bestowed on mankind by the spirit of the one true and most true God?" It was indeed just this point which in particular must be believed. Since however much I might be assaulted by calumnious questionings (and I had read much in the works of philosophers as they contradicted each other), nothing could shake these two beliefs—first, that you exist (though I did not know what your nature was), and secondly, that the government of human affairs is in your hands.

I believed this sometimes more and sometimes less strongly. Nevertheless, I always did believe that you exist and that you have a care for us, even though I did not know what to think about your substance or what way leads, or leads back, to you. So, since we were too weak to discover truth by pure reason and therefore needed the authority of Holy Writ, I now began to believe that you could not possibly have given such supreme authority to these Scriptures all over the world, unless it had been your wish that by means of them men should both believe in you and seek after you. As for the absurdities which used to offend me in Scripture, I had heard many of them explained in a convincing way and I now looked for their meanings in the depth of mystery. In fact the authority of Scripture seemed to me the more venerable and the more worthy of religious faith because, while it was easy to read for everybody, it also preserved in the more profound sense of its meaning the majesty of something secret; it offers itself to all in plain words and a very simple style of speech, yet serious thinkers have to give it their closest attention. Thus its arms are wide open to receive everyone, yet there are a few whom it draws to you along narrow ways, and these few would be fewer still if it were not for the fact that at the same time it stands on such a peak of authority and also draws crowds into its bosom because of its holy humility. These were my thoughts, and you were by me; I sighed and you heard me; I was storm tossed and you held the tiller; I was going on the broad path of this world and you did not forsake me.

6

I PANTED FOR HONORS, for money, for marriage, and you were laughing at me. I found bitterness and difficulty in following these desires, and your graciousness to me was shown in the way you would not allow me to find anything sweet which was not you. Look into my heart, Lord; for it was you who willed me to remember all this and to confess it to you. And let my soul cling to you now that you have freed it from that gripping birdlime of death! How unhappy it was then! And you pricked its wound on the quick, so that it might leave everything else and turn to you, who are above all things and without whom all things would be nothing—so that it might turn to you and be cured. I was unhappy indeed, and you made me really see my unhappiness. It was on a day when I was preparing a speech to be delivered in praise of the emperor; there would be a lot of lies in the speech, and they would be applauded by those who knew that they were lies. My heart was all wrought up with the worry of it all and was boiling in a kind of fever of melting thoughts. I was going along one of the streets of Milan when I noticed a poor beggar; he was fairly drunk, I suppose, and was laughing and enjoying himself. It was a sight which depressed me, and I spoke to the friends who were with me about all the sorrows which come to us because of our own madness. I thought of how I was toiling away, spurred on by my desires and dragging after me the load of my unhappiness and making it all the heavier by dragging it, and it seemed to me that the goal of this and all such endeavors was simply to reach a state of happiness that was free from care; the beggar had reached this state before us, and we, perhaps, might never reach it at all. With the few pennies that he had managed to beg he had actually obtained what I, by so many painful turns and such devious ways, was struggling to reach—namely, the joy of a temporary happiness.

No doubt the beggar's joy was not true joy; but it was a great deal truer than the joy which I, with my ambition, was seeking. And undoubtedly he was happy while I was worried; he was carefree while I was full of fears. And if I were asked which I would prefer, to be merry or to be frightened, I should reply "to be merry." But if I were asked next whether I would prefer to be a man like the beggar or a man like I then was myself, I should choose to be myself, worn out as I was with my cares and my fears. Was not this absurd? Was there any good reason for making such a choice? For I had no right to put myself in front of the beggar on the grounds that I was more learned than he, since I got no joy out of my learning. Instead I used it to give pleasure to men—not to teach them, only to please them. And therefore you were breaking my bones with the rod of your discipline.

So I will not allow my soul to listen to those who say to her: "The difference is in the source of a man's happiness. That beggar found his joy in being drunk, you were looking for your joy in winning glory." What glory, Lord? A glory that was not in you. For just as the beggar's joy was not true joy, so my glory was not true glory. Moreover it had a worse effect on my mind. The beggar would sleep off his drunkenness that very night; but I had gone to bed with mine and woken up with it day after day after day and I should go on doing so. Certainly it makes a difference what is the source of a man's happiness. I know it does. And the joy of a faithful hope is incomparably beyond all such vanity. Yes, and so was the beggar then beyond me; without any doubt he was the happier, not only because he was drenched in merriment while I eaten up with anxieties, but also because he by wishing people good luck had got some wine for himself while I by lying was seeking for an empty bubble of praise.

I said much along these lines to my intimate friends at the time, and I often noticed that it was the same with them as it was with me, and I found that things were not at all well with me, and I worried about it and by worrying made matters twice as bad, and if fortune seemed to smile on me at all, I felt too tired to grasp my opportunity, for it fled away almost before I could take hold of it.

7

ALL OF US who were friends together were depressed by these thoughts. The ones I talked to most about it were Alypius and Nebridius. Alypius was born in the same town as I, and his parents were important people there. He was younger than I. Indeed he had studied under me when I began teaching in our town and later in Carthage. He was very fond of me, because he thought me good and learned, and I was very fond of him because of his natural tendency toward virtue which was really remarkable in one so young. Nevertheless, he had been sucked into the whirlpool of Carthaginian bad habits, and in particular the empty enthusiasm for shows in the Circus. At the time when he was becoming involved in this wretched passion I had set up as a teacher of rhetoric there with a school open to the public, but he did not come to me as a pupil because of some difference which had arisen between his father and me. I had found out that he had got this fatal passion for the Circus and I was greatly disturbed about it, because it seemed to me that he was likely to throw away, if he had not thrown away already, all those high hopes we held of him. But I had no means of giving him advice or of using any kind of authority to restrain him; I could not appeal to his good will as a friend or to his duty as a pupil. For I thought that he shared his father's views about me. In fact he did not, and so, not allowing himself to be influenced by his father's quarrel, he began to greet me when we met and used to come into my school and sit listening for a time before going away.

Nevertheless, I had forgotten about any idea I might have had for trying to influence him so as to prevent the waste of such a good intelligence on a blind and head-strong enthusiasm for empty shows. But you, Lord, you, whose hand is on the helm of all that you have created, had not forgotten him, who was to become one day a member of your family and a high priest of your sac-rament. And his reform must quite clearly be attributed to you, as is shown by the fact that, though you brought it about by means of me, I did not know what I was doing. This was what happened. One day when I was sitting in my usual place with my pupils around me, Alypius came in and, after saluting me, sat down and listened to what was going on. In the course of my ex-position of the passage of literature with which I hap-pened to be dealing it occurred to me that I could make an apt use of a comparison taken from the games in the Circus; this would make my point clearer and more amusing, and I could combine it with some bitter sarcasm at the expense of those who were the prey of this kind of madness. You, God, know that at that time I had no thought of curing Alypius of that disease. But he took my remarks personally and believed that it was only because of him that I had made them. Another person would have taken this as a reason for being angry with me, but this fair-minded young man took it as a reason for being angry with himself and for loving me all the more. For you said long ago, and you had it put in your book: *Rebuke a wise man, and he will love thee.*

In fact I had not been rebuking him, but you make use of all men, whether or not they are aware of it, according to a method that is known to you, and that order and method is just. So out of my heart and tongue you made burning coals to cauterize and to cure that promising mind of his as it lay sick. Who can fail to praise you if he considers your mercies, mercies which I myself confess to you from the very marrow of my bones? For after those words of mine Alypius clambered out of that deep pit into which he had been glad enough to sink and in which he was being blinded by his pleasures; he took a firm hold on his mind and shook it; all the filth of the Circus fell off and he never went there again. Then he won over his father so that he might be allowed to attend my classes as a pupil. His father was unwilling enough, but gave way and gave in. Alypius was once more my pupil and became involved with me in the same superstition. He loved the Manichaean pretense of continence, considering it to be real and genuine, though in fact this kind of continence was senseless and misleading and ensnared precious souls which were not yet able to reach the depth of virtue but could easily be deceived by the superficial appearance of a virtue which was shadowy and pretended.

8

BUT THERE WAS no abandoning of the worldly career which his parents were always talking to him about. He had gone to Rome before me in order to study law and in Rome he had been quite swept away, incredibly and with a most incredible passion, by the gladiatorial shows. He was opposed to such things and detested them; but he happened to meet some of his friends and fellow pupils on their way back from dinner, and they, in spite of his protests and his vigorous resistance, used a friendly kind of violence and forced him to go along with them to the amphitheater on a day when one of these cruel and bloody shows was being presented. As he went, he said to them: "You can drag my body there, but don't imagine that you can make me turn my eyes or give my mind to the show. Though there, I shall not be there, and so I shall have the better both of you and of the show."

After hearing this his friends were all the keener to bring him along with them. No doubt they wanted to see whether he could actually do this or not. So they came to the arena and took the seats which they could find. The whole place was seething with savage enthusiasm, but he shut the doors of his eyes and forbade his soul to go out into a scene of such evil. If only he could have blocked up his ears too! For in the course of the fight some man fell; there was a great roar from the whole mass of spectators which fell upon his ears; he was overcome by curiosity and opened his eyes, feeling perfectly prepared to treat whatever he might see with scorn and to rise above it. But he then received in his soul a worse wound than that man, whom he had wanted to see, had received in his body. His own fall was more wretched than that of the gladiator which had caused all that shouting which had entered his ears and unlocked his eyes and made an opening for the thrust which was to overthrow his soul—a soul that had been reckless rather than strong and was all the weaker because it had trusted in itself when it ought to have trusted in you. He saw the blood and he gulped down savagery. Far from turning away, he fixed his eyes on it. Without knowing what was happening, he drank in madness, he was delighted with the guilty contest, drunk with the lust of blood. He was no longer the man who had come there but was one of the crowd to which he had come, a true companion of those who had brought him.

There is no more to be said. He looked, he shouted, he raved with excitement; he took away with him a madness which would goad him to come back again, and he would not only come with those who first got him there; he would go ahead of them and he would drag others with him. Yet you, with your most strong and merciful hand, rescued him from this, and you taught him to put his trust not in himself but in you. This, however, was much later.

9

NEVERTHELESS, this was already being stored up in his memory for his future healing. So also was something which happened to him when he was still a pupil of mine at Carthage. He was in the market place in the middle of the day, thinking over the words of a passage which in the ordinary course of his education he would have to say by heart. You then allowed him to be arrested by the market police as a thief, and, our God, I think that the only reason why you allowed this to happen was that one who was going to become such a great man should even then begin to learn that in cases of judging guilt man must not be too easily condemned by man on a basis of rash credulity. What happened was this: he was walking about by himself, with his notebooks and pen, in front of the law court, and just then a young man, also a student, who was the real thief, with an ax hidden under his clothes, got in (though Alypius did not see him) as far as the leaden gratings over the silversmiths' shops and began to cut away the lead. But the silversmiths underneath

heard the sound of the ax, raised the alarm, and sent
people to catch whomever they could find. Hearing their
voices the thief ran away, leaving the ax behind for fear
that he might be caught with it. Alypius had not seen the
man coming in, but he noticed him going out and saw
that he was running away fast. Wanting to know the
reason for this, he went into the place, found the ax, and
stood in front of it, wondering what it was doing there.
At this moment the men who had been sent found him,
alone and with the weapon whose noise had alarmed them
and brought them there. They seized hold of him and
dragged him off, boasting to the shopkeepers in the forum,
who came crowding around, that they had caught the
thief red-handed. And so he was led away to be handed
over to justice. But his lesson stopped here. You, Lord,
now came to the aid of his innocence, of which you were
the only witness. For as he was being led off to prison or
to torture they were met by a man who was the chief architect in charge of the public buildings. Alypius' captors
were particularly glad to meet him because they themselves were often suspected by him of making off with
property that had disappeared from the market place;
now at last, they thought, they could show him who was
really guilty. But the architect had often seen Alypius in
the house of one of the senators at which he was in the
habit of calling. He recognized him at once, took him
by the hand, got him out of the way of the mob, and
asked him what all this trouble was about. He heard
what had happened and told the crowd, who were in
a most turbulent and threatening mood, to come with
him. They went to the house of the young man who
had actually committed the crime. By the door was a
boy who was too small to imagine that anything he

might say could injure his master and who was therefore likely to tell the whole story, for he had followed
his master into the market place. Alypius recognized him
and pointed him out to the architect, who showed him
the ax and asked him whom it belonged to. The boy
at once said: "It's ours," and, after further questioning,
revealed everything. So the crime was laid at the door
of that house, much to the confusion of the crowd, who
had already begun to treat Alypius as though he were
their prisoner. He, who in the future would be a dispenser
of your word and an investigator of many cases in your
Church, went away a wiser and a more experienced man.

10

I FOUND ALYPIUS at Rome. We became very close
friends, and he came with me to Milan, partly so as not
to desert me and partly to practice the law which he
had studied—though this was rather to please his parents than because he wanted to. He had already sat three
times as an assessor and had shown an integrity which
made others wonder at him, though he himself was more
inclined to wonder at those others who could prefer gold
to honesty. His character was also tested not only by
the lure of gain but also by the threat of danger. At
Rome he was assessor to the Count of the Italian Treasury. There was at the time an extremely powerful
senator; many people were under obligations to him, and
many people were afraid of him. This man, counting upon
his usual influence, wanted to get something or other past
the courts which was in fact illegal. Alypius stood out
against it. Bribes were offered, which he treated with contempt; threats were made and he spurned them. Everyone
wondered at so rare a spirit, which neither courted the

friendship nor feared the enmity of a man who was so powerful and who was so well known for having countless means of helping people on or of doing them harm. The judge himself, in whose court Alypius sat, was also against making the concession, but he would not refuse it openly; instead he made Alypius responsible, saying that it was Alypius who was preventing him; and in fact, if he had given in, Alypius would have left the court.

One thing did tempt him, and that was his love of learning. He knew that he could have books copied for him at the cheap rate allowed to praetors. But when he considered the justice of the matter, he changed his mind for the better. Equity forbade, power allowed; he chose the former as being the more valuable. A small thing, perhaps. But *he that is faithful in little, is faithful also in much.* Nor can this be an empty word which came from the mouth of your truth: *If ye have not been faithful in the unrighteous Mammon, who will commit to your trust true riches? And if ye have not been faithful in that which is another man's, who shall give you that which is your own?*

This was the sort of person that Alypius was at that time. He was my great friend and together with me he was in a state of mental confusion as to what way of life we should take.

There was Nebridius too. He had left his native place near Carthage; he had left Carthage itself, where he usually lived; he had left his rich family estate in the country, left his home, and left his mother, since she was not prepared to follow him. He had come to Milan, and his one reason for doing so was to live with me in a most ardent search for truth and wisdom. Together with me he sighed and together with me he wavered. How he burned to discover the happy life! How keen and close was his scrutiny of the most difficult questions!

So there were together the mouths of three hungry people, sighing out their wants one to another, and *waiting upon Thee that Thou mightest give them their meat in due season.* And in all the bitterness which by your mercy followed all our worldly actions, as we looked toward the end and asked ourselves why should we suffer like this, darkness came down upon us, and we turned away in sorrow saying, *How long shall these things be?* This we said often enough, yet still we did not forsake these things, because there was no dawning gleam of a certainty to which we could hold once these things had been forsaken.

11

AND I, as I looked back over my life, was quite amazed to think of how long a time had passed since my nineteenth year, when I had first become inflamed with a passion for wisdom and had resolved that, when once I found it, I would leave behind me all the empty hopes and deceitful frenzies of vain desires. And now I was in my thirtieth year, still sticking in the same mud, still greedy for the enjoyment of things present, which fled from me and wasted me away, and all the time saying: "I shall find it tomorrow. See, it will become quite clear and I shall grasp it. Now Faustus will come and explain everything. What great men the Academics are! Is it true that no certainty can possibly be comprehended for the direction of our lives? No, it cannot be. We must look into things more carefully and not give up hope. And now see, those things in the Scriptures which used to seem absurd are not absurd; they can be understood in a different and perfectly good way. I shall take my stand where my parents placed me as a child until I can see the truth plainly. But where shall I look for it? And when shall I look for it? Ambrose has no spare time; nor have I time for reading. And where can I find the books? From where can I get them and when can I get them? Can I borrow them from anybody? I must arrange fixed periods of time and set aside certain hours for the health of my soul. A great hope has dawned. The Catholic faith does not teach the things I thought it did and vainly accused it of teaching. The learned men of that faith think it quite wrong to believe that God is bounded within the shape of a human body. Why then do I hesitate to knock, so that the rest may be laid open to me? My pupils take up all my time in the morning. But what do I do for the rest of the day? Why not do this? But, if I do, how shall I find time to call on influential friends whose support will be useful to me? When shall I prepare the lessons for which my pupils pay? When shall I have time to relax and to refresh my mind from all my preoccupations?

"But these are not the thoughts I should have. I must give up all this vanity and emptiness and devote myself entirely to the search for truth. Life is a misery, death an uncertainty. Suppose it steals suddenly upon me, in what state shall I leave this world? When can I learn what I have here neglected to learn? Shall I not be punished for my negligence? Or is it true that death will cut off and put an end to all care and all feeling? This too is something to be inquired into. But no, this cannot be true. It is not for nothing, it is not meaningless that all over the world is displayed the high and towering authority of the Christian faith. Such great and wonderful things would never have been done for us by God, if the life of the soul were to end with the death of the body. Why then do I delay? Why do I not abandon my hopes of this world and devote myself entirely to the search for God and for the happy life?

"But wait. These worldly things too are sweet; the pleasure they give is not inconsiderable; we must not be too hasty about rejecting them, because it would be a shame to go back to them again. Now think: it would not be very difficult to get some high official appointment, and then what more could I want? I have quite a number of influential friends. Not to press on too fast, I could easily get a governorship. Then I should marry a wife with money, so that she would not increase my expenses. And then I should have nothing more to desire. There have been many great men, well worth imitating, who have devoted themselves to the pursuit of wisdom and have also been married."

So I used to speak and so the winds blew and shifted and drove my heart this way and that, and time went by and I was slow in turning to the Lord. My life in you I kept on putting off from one day to the next, but I did not put off the death that daily I was dying in myself. I was in love with the idea of the happy life, but I feared to find it in its true place, and I sought for it by running away from it. I thought that I should be unbearably unhappy if I were deprived of the embraces of a woman, and I never thought of your mercy as a medicine to cure that weakness, because I had never tried it. I believed that continency was something which depended on one's own strength, and I knew that I had not enough strength for it; for I was such a fool that I did not know that it is written that no one can be continent unless you give the power. And undoubtedly you would have given it to me if with the groans of my heart I had beaten upon your ears and if in settled faith I had cast my cares upon you.

12

ALYPIUS CERTAINLY kept me from marrying. He was always saying that, if I did marry, it would be quite impossible for us to have the untroubled leisure in which we could live together in the love of wisdom, as we had so long wanted to do. With regard to all this he himself was even then quite extraordinarily chaste. When he was an adolescent he had had the experience of sexual intercourse, but, so far from becoming addicted to it, he had regretted the experience and despised it and ever since had lived in the greatest continence. As to me, I countered his arguments by producing examples of men who, though married, had pursued wisdom and served God and kept their friends and loved them faithfully. In fact I myself fell far short of their grandeur of spirit; I was the prisoner of this disease of the flesh and of its deadly sweetness, and I dragged my chain about with me, dreading the idea of its being loosed, and I pushed aside the good advice of Alypius as I might push aside the hand of one coming to unchain me which had knocked against a wound.

Also it was by means of me that the serpent began to speak to Alypius himself. My tongue was used to weave sweet snares and scatter them in his path to trap his free and unsuspecting feet. He was much surprised to find that I, of whom he thought so highly, was so stuck in the glue of this kind of pleasure that I would assert, whenever we discussed the subject, that it was quite impossible for me to live a single life. I on my side, when I saw how surprised he was, would defend myself by saying that there

was a great difference between that hurried and furtive
experience of his—which he could now scarcely remember and could thus quite easily despise—and the delights
of my normal state. If, I said, to these was added the
honorable name of marriage, he could have no reason to
be surprised that I was incapable of rejecting such a way
of life. On hearing this Alypius began to want to get married himself, not because he lusted after that kind of
pleasure, but simply for curiosity. He wanted to find out,
he said, what this thing was without which my life, which
seemed to him so pleasant, would be to me not worth
living and indeed a torment. For his mind was free of my
kind of bondage and was simply amazed at it. So from
being amazed he went on to desire the experience of it.
And he would have proceeded to the same experience and
next might well have fallen into the same slavery as that
which amazed him in me; since he wished to *make a
covenant with death,* and *he that loves danger shall fall
into it.* For neither of us had more than the faintest interest in the good and honorable side of marriage—the duty
of a controlled association and of having children. In my
case what chiefly enslaved me and kept me on tenterhooks
was the habit of sating a lust that could never be satisfied;
while he was being dragged into slavery simply by his
amazement at my behavior. So there we were until you,
most high, not forsaking our dust, but pitying our pitiful
state, came to our help in secret and wonderful ways.

13

THE MOVE TO get me married went on apace. I made
my proposal and the girl was promised to me. In all
this my mother played a large part, for, once I was
married, she wanted me to be washed in the health-

giving water of baptism for which, to her joy, she saw me becoming more fit every day, so that she now felt that her own prayers and your promises were being fulfilled in my faith. It was at my request and also to satisfy her own longing that at this time she begged you every day, crying out to you from her heart, to show her in a vision something about my future marriage; but you were never willing to do so. She did have some visual experiences of a vain and fantastical nature (caused no doubt by the eagerness of a human mind to be satisfied on this particular point), but when she told me of them, she spoke slightingly of them and not with the confidence which she always had when you were really showing her something. She used to say that there was a kind of tone or savor, impossible to define in words, by which she could tell the difference between your revelations to her and the dreams that came from her own spirit. Nevertheless, plans for my marriage went ahead and the girl was asked for. She was still about two years below the marriageable age, but I liked her and was prepared to wait.

14

A GROUP OF US, all friends together, after much thought and conversation on how we hated the whole wearisome business of human life, had almost reached the conclusion that we would retire from the crowd and live a life of peace. In order to achieve this we planned to pool our resources and make one common property out of the property of all of us. So, in the sincerity of friendship, there would be no distinction between what belonged to one man or another; all our possessions should count as one piece of property, and the whole should belong to each individual and everything should belong to everybody. It appeared that there might be about ten of us in this society and among these ten were some very rich men—Romanianus in particular, who was a fellow townsman of ours and had been a great friend of mine from childhood. He had now come to the court at Milan because of some urgent business in connection with his own affairs. He was particularly enthusiastic about the project and his voice had much weight in persuading the rest of us, since his property was much greater than anybody else's. We had decided that two of us should be, like magistrates, appointed every year to deal with the necessary provisions for life, while the rest would be left in peace. Next, however, the question was raised as to whether our wives would put up with it—some of us having wives already and I being anxious to have one. And so the whole scheme, which had been so well worked out, fell to pieces in our hands and was abandoned as impracticable. We went back to our sighing and complaining and our steps continued to follow the broad and well-worn paths of the world; for we had many thoughts in our hearts, *but Thy counsel standeth forever*. And out of this counsel you laughed ours to scorn, and you were preparing for us your own things, being about *to give us meat in due season, and to open Thy hand, and to fill our souls with blessing*.

15

MEANWHILE MY SINS were being multiplied. The woman with whom I was in the habit of sleeping was torn from my side on the grounds of being an impediment to my marriage, and my heart, which clung to her, was broken and wounded and dropping blood. She had returned to Africa after having made a vow to you that she would never go to bed with another man, and she had left with me the natural son I had had by her. But I, in my misery, could not follow the example of a woman. I had two years to wait until I could have the girl to whom I was engaged, and I could not bear the delay. So, since I was not so much a lover of marriage as a slave to lust, I found another woman for myself—not, of course, as a wife. In this way my soul's disease was fed and kept alive so that it might reach the domination of matrimony just as strong as before, or stronger, and still the slave of an unbreakable habit. Nor was the wound healed which had been made by the cutting off of my previous mistress. It burned, it hurt intensely, and then it festered, and if the pain became duller, it became more desperate.

16

PRAISE TO YOU, glory to you, fountain of mercies! As I became more unhappy, so you drew closer to me. Your right hand was ready, it was ready to drag me out of the mud and to wash me; but I did not know. And there was nothing to call me back from that deeper gulf of carnal pleasure, except the fear of death and of judgment to come, and this, whatever the opinions I held from time to time, never left my mind. I used to discuss the nature of good and evil with my friends Alypius and Nebridius, and certainly in my judgment Epicurus would have won the palm if I had not believed (as he refused to believe) that there was a life for the soul after death and treatment in accordance with its deserts. And I would put the question: "Suppose we were immortal and could live in perpetual bodily pleasure without any fear of loss, why should we not be happy, or what more could we want?" And I never realized that it was just this that made me so miserable, that in my drowned and sightless state I was unable to form an idea of the light of honor and of a beauty that is embraced for its own sake, which is invisible to the eye of flesh and can only be seen by the inner soul. I was wretched enough not to consider why and from what source it was that I found it a pleasure to discuss these ideas (shabby though they were) in the company of friends and that I could not be happy, even in the way I then understood happiness, without friends, however great might be the amount of carnal pleasure I had in addition. For certainly I loved my friends for their own sake, and I knew that they too loved me for my own sake. What tortuous ways these were, and how hopeless was the plight of my fool-hardy soul which hoped to have something better if it went away from you! It has turned indeed, over and over, on back and side and front, and always the bed was hard and you alone are rest. And, see, you are close to us, and you rescue us from our unhappy errors, and you set our feet in your way and speak kindly to us and say: "Run and I will hold you and I will bring you through and there also I will hold you."

BOOK VII

1

Now MY EVIL abominable youth was a thing of the
past. I was growing into manhood, and the older I was
the more discreditable was the emptiness of my mind.
I was unable to form an idea of any kind of substance
other than what my eyes are accustomed to see. I did
not think of you, God, in the shape of a human body.
From the moment when I began to have any knowledge of wisdom I always avoided that idea, and I was
glad that I had found the same view held in the faith
of our spiritual mother, your Catholic Church. But how
else I was to think of you, I did not know. And I, a
man, and such a man too, was trying to think of you as
the supreme, the only, the true God, and with all my
heart I believed you to be beyond the reach of corruption
and injury and change; because, though I did not know
how or whence, I still saw quite plainly and with certainty that what can be corrupted is inferior to what
cannot be corrupted, that what cannot be injured is undoubtedly to be preferred to what can be injured, and
that what suffers no change is better than what is subject to change. My heart cried out passionately against
all the phantoms I had believed in, and with this one
blow I tried to beat away from the eye of my mind all
those swarms of uncleanness which were buzzing around
it. But they only disappeared for the flickering of an eye-
lid, and then they came straight back again in a mass,
pressing on my sight and overclouding it, and the result
was that, though I did not think of you in the shape
of a human body, I was still forced to think of you as

77

a corporeal substance occupying space, whether infused into this world or diffused through the infinite space outside the world, and this substance too I regarded as being of that incorruptible, inviolable, and changeless nature which I saw as superior to the corruptible, the violable, and the mutable. And the reason was that if I tried to imagine something as not being in space it seemed to me to be nothing, and by "nothing" I mean absolutely nothing, not even a void. For if a body is taken out of its place and the place remains empty of any kind of body, whether of earth, water, air, or sky, it will still be an empty place, a "nothing" that is nevertheless in a spatial context.

So I with my gross mind (for I was not even clearly visible to myself) considered that whatever was not extended in space, whether diffused or condensed or swelling out or having some such qualities or being capable of having them, must be, in the full sense of the word, nothing. The images in my mind were like the shapes which I was used to seeing with my eyes, and I did not realize that this very act of the mind by which I formed these images was something of a different nature altogether; yet it would not be able to form the images unless it were itself something great. So, life of my life, I thought of you as an immensity through infinite space, interfused everywhere throughout the whole mass of the universe and extending beyond it in every direction for distances without end, so that the earth should have you, the sky should have you, all things should have you, and they should be bounded in you, but you should be boundless. For just as the body of the air which is above the earth does not resist the passage of the sun's light, which goes through it without breaking or cutting it, but simply by filling it entirely, so I thought that the body not only of the heaven and the air and the sea, but also of the earth, was permeable to you and, in its greatest parts as in its least, able to be penetrated so as to receive your presence and that thus a hidden kind of inspiration from within and from without governed all things which you had created.

This was the idea I formed, because I could not think in any other way. But it was false. For according to this view a greater or a lesser part of the earth would contain a greater or a lesser part of you; all things would be full of you, but in such a way that the body of an elephant would contain more of you than the body of a sparrow to the extent that it is larger and occupies more space, and thus you would be imparting your presence piecemeal to different parts of the world—small portions of you to small parts, big portions to big parts. But this is not so. However, you had not yet enlightened my darkness.

2

As to those deceived deceivers, those dumb talkers (dumb because they never uttered your Word), I had a perfectly good argument to oppose to them, and I had had it ever since the time when we were in Carthage. It was put forward by Nebridius, and all of us who heard it were much taken aback by it. There is in the Manichaean creed a sort of nation of darkness which is set up as a counter substance to you; now what, Nebridius asked, would this nation of darkness have done to you, if you had been unwilling to fight against it? If the reply was: "it would have done you some harm," then it would follow that you were capable of suffering injury and corruption. If, on the other hand, it was admitted that it could have done you no harm, then no reason could be produced why you should fight with it. Particularly when the fighting was of this kind: some portion or member of you or offspring of your own substance was supposed to become mixed with opposite powers and natures not created by you; it was then so corrupted by them and so changed for the worse as to fall from beatitude into misery and to require help so as to be delivered and cleansed; this portion of your substance was the soul, and in its state of slavery and contamination and corruption it was to receive the aid of your Word, which was free, pure, and entire. But that Word was itself corruptible because it was the offspring of one and the same substance as the soul. And so if they say that you, in your real nature —that is, in your substance by which you are—are incorruptible, then all these theories of theirs must be false and execrable, and if they say that you are corruptible, that very statement in itself, as is immediately obvious, must be false and must be abominated. This argument of Nebridius was therefore all I needed against the Manichees, whom I ought to have wholly vomited up from a stomach overcharged with them; for they had no possible answer and could not defend the way in which they thought and spoke about you without the most dreadful blasphemy of heart and tongue.

3

As to me, I would certainly say and I firmly believed that you—our Lord, the true God, who made not only our souls but our bodies, and not only our souls and bodies but all men and all things—were undefilable and unalterable and in no way to be changed, and yet I still could not understand clearly and distinctly what was the cause of evil. Whatever it might be, however, I did realize that my inquiry must not be carried out along lines which would lead me to believe that the immutable God was mutable; if I did that, I should become myself the very evil which I was looking for. And so I pursued the inquiry without anxiety, being quite certain that what the Manichees said was not true. I had turned against them with my whole heart, because I saw that in their inquiries into the origin of evil they were full of evil themselves; for they preferred to believe that your substance could suffer evil rather than that their substance could do evil.

And I made an effort to understand what I had heard, that free will is the cause of our doing evil and your just judgment the cause of our suffering it; but I could not grasp this clearly. And so, though I tried to raise the eyes of my mind from the pit, I fell back into it again and as often as I tried so often did I fall back. But I was a little raised up toward your light by the fact that I was just as certain that I had a will as that I had a life. So, when I willed to do or not to do something, I was perfectly certain that the act of willing was mine and not anybody else's, and I was now getting near to the conclusion that here was the cause of my sin.

But with regard to things which I did unwillingly, it seemed to me that I was suffering rather than doing, and I considered such things to be my punishment rather than my fault; though, as I thought of you as just, I was quick to admit that I was not being punished unjustly. But then I asked: "Who made me? Was it not my God, who is not only good but goodness itself? How then could it be that I should will evil and refuse my assent to good, so that it would be just for me to be punished?

Who was it who set and ingrafted in me this plant of bitterness, seeing that I was wholly made by my most sweet God? If the devil is responsible, then where did the devil come from? And if it was by his own perverse will that the devil himself, after having been a good angel, became a devil, then what was the origin in him of the evil will by which he became a devil, seeing that he was made all angel by the all-good creator?" By these thoughts I was thrust down again and choked; but I was not brought down so low as to that hell of error where no one confesses to you and where it is believed that you suffer evil rather than that man does evil.

4

So I STRUGGLED ON to find out the rest in the same way as I had already discovered that the incorruptible is better than the corruptible, and therefore I was ready to confess that, whatever your nature might be, you must be incorruptible. For no soul ever has been or ever will be able to conceive of anything better than you, who are the supreme and the best good. And, since in all truth and certainty the view which I now held—that the incorruptible is to be preferred to the corruptible—was right, I should have been able, if you had not been incorruptible, to have reached in imagination something better than my God. It was here, therefore—in my knowledge that the incorruptible was better than the corruptible—that I ought to have been looking for you, and I should have gone on from here to discover where evil is, that is to say, what is the origin of that corruption by which your own substance cannot possibly be affected. For there is absolutely no way in which corruption can affect our God, neither by will nor by necessity nor by

evil is not something real and positive but rather a privation of good

accident; because He Himself is God and what He wills is good and He Himself is goodness; but to be corrupted is not good. Nor are you forced toward anything against your will, for your will is not greater than your power. But it would be greater, if you were greater than yourself. For the will and power of God is God Himself. And how could any accident surprise you, who know all things? There is nothing in existence except as a result of your knowing it. But what need is there of more words to show that the substance which is God is not corruptible? If it were, it would not be God.

5

I SEARCHED FOR the origin of evil, and I searched for it in an evil way, and I did not see the evil in the very method of my search. I put the whole creation in front of the eyes of my spirit, both what was visible— like earth, sea, air, stars, trees, and mortal creatures— and what was invisible—like the firmament of the heaven above and all the angels and spiritual beings there. Though even these spiritual beings I conceived of as bodies, each in its imagined place. And I thought of all your creation as one great mass, distinguished in accordance with the kinds of bodies of which it was made up, some being real bodies, others the kind of bodies which I imagined instead of spirits. I thought of this mass as being of an enormous size, not the size which it actually was (which I could not know), but the size which seemed to me convenient; though I conceived of it as being finite on every side. And I thought of you, Lord, as surrounding it on every side and penetrating it, but being in all directions infinite. It was as though there were a sea, which everywhere and on all sides through immensity was just one infinite sea, but which had inside it a sponge which, though very big, was still bounded. This sponge of course would in all its parts be completely filled with the immeasurable sea. So I thought of your creation as finite and as filled with you, who were infinite. And I said: "Here is God, and here is what God has created; and God is good and is most mightily and incomparably better than all these. Yet He, being good, created them good, and see how He surrounds them and fills them. Where, then, is evil? Where did it come from and how did it creep in here? What is its root and seed? Or does it simply not exist? In that case why do we fear and take precautions against something that does not exist? Or if there is no point in our fears, then our fears themselves are an evil which goads and tortures the heart for no good reason—and all the worse an evil if there is nothing to be afraid of and we are still afraid. Therefore, either there is evil which we fear or else the fact that we do fear is evil. Where then does evil come from, seeing that God is good and made all things good? Certainly it was the greater and supreme Good who made these lesser goods, yet still all are good, both the creator and his creation. Where then did evil come from? Or was there some evil element in the material of creation, and did God shape and form it, yet still leave in it something which He did not change into good? But why? Being omnipotent, did He lack the power to change and transform the whole so that no trace of evil should remain? Indeed why should He choose to use such material for making anything? Would He not rather, with this same omnipotence, cause it not to exist at all? Could it exist against His will? Or, supposing it was eternal, why for so long through all the infinite spaces of time past did He allow it to exist and then so much later

decide to make something out of it? Or, if He did suddenly decide on some action, would not the omnipotent
prefer to act in such a way that this evil material should
cease to exist, and that He alone should be, the whole,
true, supreme, and infinite Good? Or, since it was not
good that He who was good should frame and create
something not good, then why did He not take away and
reduce to nothing the material that was evil and then
Himself provide good material from which to create all
things? For He would not be omnipotent if He could not
create something good without having to rely on material
which He had not Himself created."

These were the kind of thoughts which I turned over
and over in my unhappy heart, a heart overburdened
with those biting cares that came from my fear of death
and my failure to discover the truth. Yet the faith of your
Christ, our Lord and Saviour, professed in the Catholic
Church, remained steadfastly fixed in my heart, even
though it was on many points still unformed and swerving
from the right rule of doctrine. But, nevertheless, my
mind did not abandon it, but rather drank more and more
deeply of it every day.

6

BY THIS TIME TOO I had rejected the fallacious fore-
casts and impious ravings of the astrologers. Here also,
my God, let your own mercies make confession to you
from the very depths of my soul. For this was entirely
due to you. Who else is it who calls us back from the
death of error, except the life that does not know death,
and the wisdom which, needing no light, enlightens minds
which are in darkness, that wisdom by which the whole
world, even to the leaves of trees drifting in the wind, is

governed? So it was you who dealt with that obstinate state of mind in which I was when I argued with that sharp-witted old man Vindicianus and with the young Nebridius, with his fine spiritual qualities. Vindicianus used to maintain most energetically, and Nebridius, though with rather more hesitation, often used to say too that the supposed art of foretelling the future was no art at all; it was rather the case that the guesses people made had the luck of a lottery; those who made a number of predictions would make some that turned out true, though in making them no knowledge was shown; it was simply a question of saying so many things that in the course of it one was bound to stumble on something true. And then, again by your provision, I had a friend who was a very keen follower of the astrologers. He had no great knowledge of their literature but was, as I said, one who showed considerable curiosity about them. He did know something, however, which he said had been told him by his father; but he did not know how useful this information was for the overthrowing of any belief one might have in astrology. The man's name was Firminus; he had had a good education and was thoroughly trained in rhetoric. As he considered me a great friend he asked me to give him my advice about some affairs of his which greatly concerned his worldly ambitions, and he wanted to know what I thought about his so-called "constellations" in the matter. By this time I was beginning to come around to the views of Nebridius about astrology, but I did not refuse to make my conjectures and to tell Firminus how (uncertain as I was) things seemed to me. I added however that I was now practically certain that all these inquiries were a ridiculous waste of time. He then told me about his father, who had been a great stu-

dent of astrology and had had a friend who was equally
enthusiastic and had joined him in his studies. They
studied zealously and compared notes and their hearts became so much on fire with this nonsense that they used to
make careful observations of the exact times when even
the dumb animals in their houses gave birth and they
noted the position of the heavens at these times—all in
order to collect experimental evidence for this presumed
art. Firminus said that his father had told him that at the
time when his mother was pregnant with him a female
slave belonging to this friend of his father's was also
about to have a child. This of course was known to the
woman's master, who, even when one of his bitches was
having puppies, would be most meticulously careful to
find out all about it. So now in the case of this slave of his
he was taking the most careful and thorough notes with
regard to days, hours, and the smallest fractions of hours,
while Firminus' father was doing just the same thing with
regard to his wife. It happened that the two women had
their babies at the same moment, so that for each new-
born child the men were forced to cast exactly the same
horoscope down to the last detail, one for his son, the
other for the little slave. For as soon as the women's labor
began each friend had let the other know what was going
on in his house and they had messengers ready to send to
each other as soon as it was known that one or other of
the children had been born—and, since the births were
taking place in their own households, they would know at
once. Firminus said that the messengers sent by each
met exactly halfway between the two houses, so that it
was impossible for either of the men to have made any
different observations from the other one with regard to
the position of the stars or the precise moment of time.

Yet Firminus, born to wealth in his parents' house, had one of the brighter careers in life; his riches increased and he held distinguished positions; whereas the slave had no alleviation in the burden of his condition; he continued to serve his masters. So Firminus, who knew him, told me.

After hearing this story and (since Firminus was a perfectly reliable witness) believing it, all my previous resistance gave way and collapsed. First I attempted to induce Firminus himself to give up this form of curiosity by telling him that if I had had to consult his stars in order to give him a true forecast of the future, I certainly ought to have seen in them that his parents were people of distinction, that his family was a noble one in his own city, that he was born free, and that he had had a good and liberal education. But if that slave had asked me for my opinion and I had consulted his stars, which were exactly the same as those under which Firminus was born, then I ought to have seen in them that his family was of the very lowest, that he was a slave, and that in every other respect he had a completely different lot in life from that of Firminus. It followed, therefore, that, after inspecting the same stars, I must, if I were to tell the truth, say different things in the two cases, for if I were to say the same things, it would be a falsehood, and from this it appeared to me quite certain that anything true which may be said after casting a horoscope is true by luck and not by skill, and anything false is false not because of any lack of skill in the art but simply because the luck has gone the other way.

With this approach to the subject I began to look more deeply into the same kind of argument in case one of those fools who make money out of astrology, and whom

I was already longing to challenge and to make laughing-stocks of, was to object by saying that what Firminus had told me or what his father had told him was untrue. So I considered the cases of those who are born twins. Most of them come from the womb very close to each other, and the small interval of time between the two births (whatever influence these people may pretend it has in reality) simply cannot be noted by any human method of observation so as to be put down in the tables which the astrologer must look at in order to foretell the truth. And of course it will not be the truth. After looking at the same figures an astrologer would have had to predict the same futures for Esau and for Jacob; but in fact the same things did not happen to them. Either, then, he would have to have made a false prediction, or else, if his prediction was true, it would have to have been different in each case; yet each case was based on the same figures. So, if he did tell the truth, it would be by luck and not by skill. For you, Lord, the most just controller of the universe, act in your own secret way so that, while neither he who consults nor he who is consulted knows what is being done, still when a man consults he is told out of the abyss of your just judgment what, in accordance with the secret deservings of souls, he ought to be told. Let no man say to you "What is this?" or "Why is this?" He must not, he must not say such things. For he is a man.

7

AND SO, MY HELPER, you had set me free from those chains. But still I asked: "What is the origin of evil?" and I could find no answer. Yet in all the fluctuations of my thought you did not allow me to be carried away from the faith in which I believed that you existed, that your substance was unchangeable, that you had care for men, and that you would judge them; also that in Christ your Son our Lord and in the Holy Scriptures approved by the authority of your Catholic Church you had laid down the way of man's salvation to the life which is to come after death. With these beliefs firmly and irrevocably rooted in my mind I sought, in a kind of passion, the answer to the question: "What is the origin of evil?" What agonies I suffered, what groans, my God, came from my heart in its labor! And you were listening, though I did not know it. When in silence I strongly urged my question, the quiet contrition of my soul was a great cry to your mercy. You knew what I was suffering, and no man knew it. For how little there was of it which I could put into words even for the hearing of my most intimate friends! How could they hear the tumult of my soul when I had neither time nor language sufficient to express it? Yet all of it reached your hearing, all the roarings and groanings of my heart, and my desire was in front of you and the light of my eyes was not with me. For that light was within and I was out of doors; that was not in space, but my mind was intent on things which were in space, and I could find no place there to rest, and the things of space did not welcome me so that I could say: "It is enough, it is well," nor did they let me go back to where it would have been well enough with me. For I was superior to them, but inferior to you. You are my true joy and I am subject to you, and you have subjected to me the things in your creation which are below me. And this was the correct admixture, the middle way for my salvation—that I should remain in your image and, by serving you, be master of the body. But when I arrogantly rose up against you and *ran upon my Lord with my neck, with the thick bosses of my buckler,* even these inferior things became above me and kept me under, and there was no loosening of their hold and no chance of breathing. When I opened my eyes they swarmed around me from all sides in clouds, and when I tried to think, these corporeal images stood in my way and prevented me from returning to you. It was as though they were saying: "Where are you going to, you unworthy and unclean creature?" All this had grown out of my wound; for you humble the proud like one who is wounded, and I was separated from you by the swelling of my pride. It was as though my cheeks had swollen up so that I could not see out of my eyes.

8

BUT YOU, LORD, abide forever, and you are not angry with us forever because you have pity on our dust and ashes, and it was pleasing in your sight to reform my deformity. Inside me your good was working on me to make me restless until you should become clear and certain to my inward sight. Through the hidden hand of your healing art my swelling abated and from day to day the troubled and clouded sight of my mind grew better through the stinging ointment of a healthy sorrow.

9

FIRST YOU WISHED to show me how *Thou resistest the proud but givest grace to the humble* and how great was your mercy in showing to men the way of humility in that the Word was made flesh and dwelt among men. And so by means of a man I knew (he was an extraordinarily conceited person) you brought to my notice some books written by the Platonists, which had been translated from

Greek into Latin. In these books I found it stated, not of course in the same words but to precisely the same effect and with a number of different sorts of reasons, that: *In the beginning was the Word, and the Word was with God, and the Word was God: the Same was in the beginning with God: all things were made by Him, and without Him was nothing made: that which was made by Him is life, and the life was the light of men, and the light shineth in the darkness, and the darkness comprehended it not.* Also that the soul of man, though it *bears witness to the light,* yet itself *is not that light;* but the Word, God Himself, *is that true light that lighteth every man that cometh into the world.* Also that *He was in the world, and the world was made by Him, and the world knew Him not.* But I did not find in the books of the Platonists that: *He came unto His own, and His own received Him not; but as many as received Him, to them gave He power to become the sons of God, as many as believed in His name.*

I also read in these books that God the Word was *born not of flesh nor of blood, nor of the will of man, nor of the will of the flesh, but of God.* But I did not find then that *the Word was made flesh and dwelt among us.* I did discover, as I examined these books, that it was stated in a number of different ways that *the Son was in the form of the Father, and thought it not robbery to be equal with God,* because by nature He was God. But one will not find in the writings of the Platonists that *He emptied Himself, taking the form of a servant, being made in the likeness of men, and found in fashion as a man, humbled Himself, and became obedient unto death, even the death of the cross: wherefore God exalted Him from the dead, and gave Him a name above every name, that at the*

*name of Jesus every knee should bow, of things in heaven,
and things in earth, and things under the earth; and that
every tongue should confess that the Lord Jesus is in the
glory of God the Father.*

I did find there that your only-begotten Son was before
all times and beyond all times and remains unchangeable,
coeternal with you, and that *of His fullness souls receive,*
that they may be blessed; also that by participation of the
wisdom that abides in them they are renewed so as to become wise. But I did not find that *in due time He died
for the ungodly,* or that *Thou sparedst not Thine only
Son, but deliveredst Him for us all.* For *Thou hiddest
these things from the wise, and revealedst them to babes;*
so that they *that labor and are heavy laden might come
unto Him and He refresh them,* because *He is meek and
lowly in heart, and the meek He directeth in judgment,
and the gentle He teacheth His ways, beholding our low-
liness and trouble, and forgiving all our sins.* But those
who, like actors on the stage, are raised up above the
general level in their supposedly superior learning do not
hear him saying: *Learn of Me, for I am meek and lowly
in heart, and ye shall find rest to your souls. Although
they knew God, yet they glorify Him not as God, nor
are thankful, but wax vain in their thoughts, and their
foolish heart is darkened; professing that they were wise,
they became fools.*

I read there too that they had *changed the glory of Thy
incorruptible nature* into idols and images of various
kinds, *into the likeness of the image of corruptible man,
and birds and beasts and creeping things,* indeed into that
Egyptian food for which Esau lost his birthright, since
that people which was your firstborn worshiped the head
of a four-footed beast instead of you, turning in their

hearts back to Egypt, and bowing down their soul, your image, in front of the image of a *calf that eateth hay.* I found these things here, but I did not feed on them. For it pleased you, Lord, to take away the reproach of inferiority from Jacob and to cause the elder to serve the younger, and you have called the Gentiles into your inheritance. I myself had come to you from the Gentiles, and I thought of the gold which you willed that your people should carry away from Egypt, since it was yours wherever it was. And you had said to the Athenians by your apostle that *in Thee we live and move and have our being, as certain of their own poets had said,* and for sure these books that I was reading came from Athens. But I did not set my mind on the idols of the Egyptians *which they served with the gold that was yours, changing the truth of God into a lie and worshiping and serving the creature more than the creator.*

10

I WAS ADMONISHED by all this to return to my own self, and, with you to guide me, I entered into the innermost part of myself, and I was able to do this because you were my helper. I entered and I saw with my soul's eye (such as it was) an unchangeable light shining above this eye of my soul and above my mind. It was not the ordinary light which is visible to all flesh, nor something of the same sort, only bigger, as though it might be our ordinary light shining much much more brightly and filling everything with its greatness. No, it was not like that; it was different, entirely different from anything of the kind. Nor was it above my mind as oil floats on water or as the heaven is above the earth. It was higher than I, because it made me, and I was lower because I was made by it. He who knows truth knows that light, and he who knows that light knows eternity. Love knows it. O eternal truth and true love and beloved eternity! You are my God; to you I sigh by day and by night. And when I first knew you, you raised me up so that I could see that there was something to see and that I still lacked the ability to see it. And you beat back the weakness of my sight, blazing upon me with your rays, and I trembled in love and in dread, and I found that I was far distant from you, in a region of total unlikeness, as if I were hearing your voice from on high saying: "I am the food of grown men. Grow and you shall feed upon me. And you will not, as with the food of the body, change me into yourself, but you will be changed into me." And I learned that *Thou, for iniquity, chastenest man and Thou madest my soul to consume away like a spider*. And I said: "Is truth therefore nothing because it is not extended through any kind of space, whether finite or infinite?" And from far away you cried out to me: "I am that I am." And I heard, as one hears things in the heart, and there was no longer any reason at all for me to doubt. I would sooner doubt my own existence than the existence of that truth *which is clearly seen being understood by those things which are made*.

11

AND I CONSIDERED the other things which are below you, and I saw that, in a complete sense, they neither are nor are not in existence. They are, since they are from you; they are not, since they are not what you are. For that which truly is, is that which remains unchangeably. *It is good then for me to hold fast unto God;* because if I do not remain in Him, I shall not be able to remain in myself. But He, remaining in Himself, renews all things. And *Thou art my Lord, since Thou standest not in need of my goodness.*

12

AND IT BECAME clear to me that things which are subject to corruption are good. They would not be subject to corruption if they were either supremely good or not good at all; for, if they were supremely good, they would be incorruptible, and, if there was nothing good in them, there would be nothing which could be corrupted. For corruption does harm, and, unless what is good in a thing is diminished, no harm could be done. Therefore, either corruption does no harm (which is impossible), or (which is quite certain) all things which suffer corruption are deprived of something good in them. Supposing them to be deprived of all good, they will cease to exist altogether. For, if they continue to exist and can no longer be corrupted, they will be better than before, because they will be permanently beyond the reach of corruption. What indeed could be more monstrous than to assert that things could become better by losing all their goodness? So if they are deprived of all good, they will cease to exist altogether. Therefore, so long as they exist, they are good. Therefore, all things that are, are good, and as to that evil, the origin of which I was seeking for, it is not a substance, since, if it were a substance, it would be good. For it would either have to be an incorruptible substance (which is the highest form of goodness) or else a corruptible substance (which, unless it had good in it, could not be corruptible). So I saw plainly and clearly that you have made all things good, nor are there any substances at all which you have not

made. And because you did not make all things equal,
therefore they each and all have their existence; because
they are good individually, and at the same time they
are altogether very good, because our God *made all
things very good.*

13

To YOU, THEN, there is no such thing at all as evil. And
the same is true not only of you but of your whole
creation, since there is nothing outside it to break in
and corrupt the order which you have imposed on it.
But in some of its parts there are some things which are
considered evil because they do not harmonize with other
parts; yet with still other parts they do harmonize and
are good and they are good in themselves. And all these
things which do not fit in with each other do fit in with
that lower part of creation which we call the earth, which
has its own cloudy and windy sky which again is fitting to
it. Far be it that I should say: "I wish these things did not
exist," because even if these were the only things I saw,
though certainly I should long for something better yet,
still for these things alone I ought to praise you; for
things from the earth show that you are to be praised—
*dragons, and all deeps, fire, hail, snow, ice, and stormy
wind, which fulfill Thy Word; mountains, and all hills,
fruitful trees and all cedars; beasts and all cattle, creeping
things and flying fowls; kings of the earth, and all people,
princes and all judges of the earth; young men and
maidens, old men and young, praise Thy name.* And since
from the heavens these *praise Thee, praise Thee, our
God, in the heights, all Thy angels, all Thy hosts, sun
and moon, all the stars and light, the heaven of heavens,
and the waters that be above the heavens, praise Thy*

name. So I no longer desired better things. I had envisaged all things in their totality, and, with a sounder judgment, I realized that, while higher things are certainly better than lower things, all things together are better than the higher things by themselves.

14

IT IS THE MARK of an unsound mind to be displeased with any single thing in your creation, and so it was with me, when I was displeased with many of the things which you made. And because my soul did not dare to be displeased with my God, I refused to admit that whatever did displease it was yours. And from this point it had gone on to hold the view that there are two substances, and here it found no rest and only talked perversely. And next it had gone back again and made for itself a God to fill the infinite distances of all space, and it had imagined this God to be you and had placed it in its own heart, thus again becoming the temple of its own idol, a temple abominable to you. But you, though I was not aware of it, laid your kindly hand upon my head and covered up my eyes so that they should not see vanity, and then I relaxed a little from myself, and sleep fell upon my madness. And I woke up in you and saw you infinite in a different way, and that sight was not from the eyes of the flesh.

15

AND I LOOKED AT other things and saw that they owe their existence to you and are all bounded in you, not in a spatial sense, but because your being contains everything in the hand of your truth, and all things are true insofar as they exist, and the only meaning of falsehood

is when something is thought to exist when it does not.
And I saw that all things fitted in not only with their
places but with their times, and that you, who alone
are eternal, did not begin to work after the passage of
innumerable spaces of time, since all spaces of time, both
past and future, could neither go nor come without your
permanent presence and operation.

16

I KNEW FROM my own experience that there is nothing strange in the fact that a sick person will find uneat-
able the same bread which a healthy person enjoys, or
that good eyes love the light and bad eyes hate it. Your
justice too displeases the wicked, and even more dis-
pleasing are vipers and reptiles, though you created them
good and well fitted to the lower parts of your creation,
and to these lower parts of creation the wicked themselves are well fitted and become the better fitted the
more they are unlike you, although in becoming more like
you they will become better fitted to the higher parts of
your creation. And I asked: "What is wickedness?" and
found that it is not a substance but a perversity of the
will turning away from you, God, the supreme substance,
toward lower things—casting away, as it were, its own
insides, and swelling with desire for what is outside it.

17

AND I FELT wonder at the thought that now I loved
you and not a phantom instead of you. But I did not stay
in the enjoyment of my God; I was swept away to you
by your own beauty, and then I was torn away from you
by my own weight and fell back groaning toward these
lower things. Carnal habit was this weight. But there re-

mained with me the memory of you; I knew with certainty that it was to you that I must cling, but I knew too that I was not yet capable of doing so; because *the body which is corrupted, presseth down the soul, and the earthly tabernacle weighteth down the mind that museth upon many things.* I was perfectly sure of this, *that Thy invisible works from the creation of the world are clearly seen, being understood by the things that are made, even Thy eternal power and Godhead.* For I considered how it was that I recognized the beauty of bodies, whether in the heaven or on earth, and what criterion I had to make a correct judgment of changing things and to say: "This is as it should be, this is not." So, as I considered how it was that I came to make these judgments which I did make, I had discovered that above my changing mind was the unchangeable and true eternity of truth. And so I went on by stages from bodies to the soul which perceives by means of the bodily senses, and from this to the inner power of the soul to which the bodily senses present external things. The faculties of animals extend as far as this, and from this point I went on to the faculty of reason to which sense data are referred for judgment. This also found itself in me to be something subject to change. It then, as it were, raised itself up to the level of its own understanding, freed my thought from the power of habit, and withdrew itself from those crowds of contradictory phantasms, so that it might discover what was that light with which it was illumined when, without the least hesitation, it cried out that the unchangeable is to be preferred to the changeable, and how it was that it had knowledge of the unchangeable itself: for unless it had knowledge in some way of the unchangeable, it could in no way prefer it with certainty to the changeable. And then, in the flash of a trembling glance, my mind arrived at That Which Is. Now indeed I saw your *invisible things understood by the things which are made,* but I had not the power to keep my eye steadily fixed; in my weakness I felt myself falling back and returning again to my habitual ways, carrying nothing with me except a loving memory of it and a longing for something which may be described as a kind of food of which I had perceived the fragrance but which I was not yet able to eat.

18

AND I TRIED to find a way of gaining the strength necessary for enjoying you, and I could not find it until I embraced that *Mediator betwixt God and men, the Man Christ Jesus, who is over all, God blessed for evermore,* calling to me and saying, *I am the way, the truth and the life,* and mingling with our flesh that food which I lacked strength to take; for *the Word was made flesh,* so that your wisdom, by which you created all things, might give its milk to our infancy.

I was not humble enough to possess Jesus in His humility as my God, nor did I know what lesson was taught by His weakness. For your Word, the eternal truth, high above the highest parts of your creation, raises up to Itself those who are subdued; but in this lower world He built for Himself a humble dwelling out of our clay, by means of which He might detach from themselves those who were to be subdued and bring them over to Himself, healing the swelling of their pride and fostering their love, so that instead of going further in their own self-confidence they should put on weakness, seeing at their feet divinity in the weakness that it had put on by

wearing our "coat of skin"; and then, weary, they should
cast themselves down upon that divinity which, rising,
would bear them up aloft.

19

BUT THIS WAS NOT the way I thought then. I thought
of my Lord Christ simply as a man of the very highest
wisdom, whom no one could equal; and in particular it
seemed to me that His miraculous birth from a virgin—
as an example of how temporal things should be despised
for the sake of obtaining immortality—showed such divine care for us that He deserved full authority over us as
a master. But I had not the faintest notion of the mystery
contained in "The Word was made flesh." All that I had
gathered from the written tradition about Him (accounts
of how He ate, drank, slept, walked, was glad, was sad,
preached) led me to believe that His flesh had only
become united with your Word by means of a human
soul and a human mind. This must be known to everyone
who knows the immutability of your Word, and I, within
the limits of my capacity, did now know this without
having any doubt about it at all. For to be now moving
and now not moving the limbs of the body by an act of
will, to be now feeling some emotion and now not feeling it, to be at one moment uttering wisdom by means
of the signs of speech and at the next moment to be silent
—these are all marks of a soul and a mind which are
mutable. And if the written tradition about Him were
false on these points, all the rest too would come under
suspicion of falsehood, and there would be no sure faith
in Scripture left for mankind. And so, since what is written
in Scripture is true, I recognized in Christ a complete
man; not merely with a man's body or with the body and

soul of a man and not a man's mind, but altogether a man, and I thought that He was to be preferred to others, not because He was Truth in person, but because of the exceptional qualities of His human nature and His more perfect participation in wisdom.

Alypius, on the other hand, thought that the Catholic belief in a God clothed in flesh meant that in Christ there were God and the flesh, but not the soul; he did not think that they ascribed to Him a human mind. And since he was convinced that the actions recorded of Christ could only have been done by a vital and rational creature, his way toward the Christian faith itself was all the more laborious. Later he realized that this was the error of the Apollinarian heretics and he came over joyfully to the Catholic faith. As to me, I must admit that it was only some time afterward that I learned how in the understanding of "The Word was made flesh" Catholic truth is distinguished from the false view of Photinus. Indeed by proving heretics to be wrong we bring into clearer light what your Church believes and what sound doctrine is. *For there must also be heresies, that the approved may be made manifest among the weak.*

20

BUT THEN, after reading these books of the Platonists which taught me to seek for a truth which was incorporeal, I came to see your *invisible things, understood by those things which are made.* I fell back again from this point, but still I had an apprehension of what, through the darkness of my mind, I was not able to contemplate; I was certain that you are and that you are infinite, yet not in the sense of being diffused through space whether infinite or finite: that you truly are, and

are always the same, not in any part or by any motion
different or otherwise: also that all other things are
from you, as is proved most certainly by the mere fact
that they exist. On all these points I was perfectly certain,
but I was still too weak to be able to enjoy you. I talked
away as if I were a finished scholar; but, if I had not
sought the way to you in Christ our Saviour, what would
have been finished would have been my soul. For I had
begun to want to have the reputation of a wise man; my
punishment was within me, but I did not weep; I was
merely puffed up with my knowledge. Where was that
charity which builds from the foundation of humility, the
foundation which is Christ Jesus? Humility was not a
subject which those books would ever have taught me.
Yet I believe that you wanted me to come upon these
books before I made a study of your Scriptures. You
wanted the impression made by them on me to be printed
in my memory, so that when later I had become, as it
were, tamed by your books (your fingers dressing my
wounds), I should be able to see clearly what the difference is between presumption and confession, between
those who see their goal without seeing how to get there
and those who see the way which leads to that happy
country which is there for us not only to perceive but to
live in. For if I had been first trained in your Scriptures
and by my familiarity with them had found you growing
sweet to me, and had then afterward come upon these
books of the Platonists, it is possible that they might have
swept me away from the solid basis of piety; or, even
if I had held firmly to that healthy disposition which
I had imbibed, I might have thought that the same
disposition could be acquired by someone who had read
only the Platonic books.

21

So I MOST GREEDILY seized upon the venerable writings of your spirit and in particular the works of the apostle Paul. In the past it had sometimes seemed to me that he contradicted himself and that what he said conflicted with the testimonies of the law and the prophets; but all these difficulties had now disappeared; I saw one and the same face of pure eloquence and learned *to rejoice with trembling.* Having begun, I discovered that everything in the Platonists which I had found true was expressed here, but it was expressed to the glory of your grace; so that whoever sees should not *so glory as if he had not received*—received, indeed, not only what he sees but also the power to see it; for *what hath he, which he hath not received.* I found too that one is not only instructed so as to see you, who are the same forever, but also so as to grow strong enough to lay hold on you, and he who cannot see you for the distance, may yet walk along the road by which he will arrive and see you and lay hold on you. For, though a man *be delighted with the law of God after the inner man,* what shall he do about that *other law in his members which warreth against the law of his mind, and bringeth him into captivity to the law of sin, which is in his members?* For, *Thou art righteous, O Lord, but we have sinned and committed iniquity, and have done wickedly,* and your hand has grown heavy upon us, and we have justly been handed over to that ancient sinner, the president of death; because he persuaded our will to be like his will, whereby he did not stand in your truth. *What shall wretched man do? Who shall deliver him from the body of this death, but only Thy Grace,* through Jesus *Christ, our Lord,* whom

in love and favor of God

you have begotten coeternal and *formedst in the beginning of Thy ways, in whom the prince of this world found nothing worthy of death,* yet killed him, and *the handwriting, which was contrary to us, was blotted out.*

None of this is to be found in the books of the Platonists. Their pages make no mention of the face and look of pity, the tears of confession, your *sacrifice—a troubled spirit, a broken and a contrite heart,* the salvation of the people, *the bridal city, the earnest of the Holy Ghost, the cup of our redemption.* No one sings there, *Shall not my soul be submitted unto God? For of Him cometh my salvation. For He is my God and my salvation, my guardian, I shall no more be moved.* No one there hears him call, *Come unto Me all ye that labor.* They are too proud to *learn of Him, because He is meek and lowly of heart; for these things hast Thou hid from the wise and prudent, and hast revealed them unto babes.* It is one thing to see from a mountaintop in the forests the land of peace in the distance and not to find the way to it and to struggle in vain along impassable tracks, ambushed and beset on all sides by fugitive deserters under their chief *the Lion and the Dragon,* and it is another thing to hold to the way that leads there, a road built and guarded by our heavenly General, where no banditry is committed by deserters from the celestial army; for they avoid it like the plague. In marvelous ways these things grew and fixed themselves in the depths of my being as I read that *least of Thy apostles,* and had meditated upon your works and had trembled.

BOOK VIII

1

MY GOD, let me remember with thanks and let me confess to you your mercies done to me. Let my bones be penetrated with your love and let them say: *Who is like unto Thee, O Lord? Thou hast broken my bonds in sunder, I will offer unto Thee the sacrifice of thanksgiving.* I will tell how it was that you broke my bonds, and all your worshipers who hear this will say: "Blessed be the Lord in heaven and in earth, great and wonderful is His name."

Your words had stuck in my heart and *I was hedged around about on all sides by Thee.* Of your eternal life I was now certain, although I had seen it in an enigma and *as through a glass.* But I had ceased to have any doubt that there was an incorruptible substance from which came every substance. I no longer desired to be more certain of you, only to stand more firmly in you.

In my own temporal life everything was unsettled and *my heart had to be purged from the old leaven.* The way—the Saviour Himself—pleased me; but I was still reluctant to enter its narrowness. It was you who put the idea into my mind (and the idea seemed good to me) to go to Simplicianus. He seemed to me a good servant of yours and your grace shone in him. I had heard too that from his youth he had lived a life devoted to you. He had now grown old, and it seemed to me that he must have experienced much and learned much as a result of having lived so long in so earnestly following your way, and so indeed he had. So, after telling him of my troubles, I wanted him to make use of his experience and learning in

107

order to show me the best means by which someone feeling as I did could set his foot on your way.

For I saw the Church full, and one went this way, and another that way. But I was displeased with the worldly life which I was leading. It was a really great burden to me and to help me bear such a heavy form of slavery I no longer had the impulse and encouragement of my old hopes and desires for position and wealth. Compared with your sweetness and the beauty of your house, which I loved, these things no longer pleased me. But I was still closely bound by my need of woman. Not that the apostle forbade me to marry, although he might recommend something better, his great wish being that all men should be as he was. But I lacked the strength and was inclined to choose the softer place, and because of this one thing everything else with me was in confusion; I was tired out and wasted away with gnawing anxieties, because I was compelled to put up with all sorts of things which I did not want simply because they were inseparable from that state of living with a wife to which I was utterly and entirely bound. I had heard from the mouth of Truth that *there were some eunuchs, which had made themselves eunuchs for the Kingdom of heaven's sake; but,* he says, *let him who can receive it, receive it. Surely vain are all men who are ignorant of God, and could not out of the good things which are seen, find out Him who is good.* But I was no longer in that kind of vanity; I had gone beyond it, and, by the common witness of all creation, I had found you, our Creator, and your Word, God with you, and one God together with you, by whom you created all things. But there is also another kind of impiety, that of those *who knowing God, glorified Him not as God, neither were thankful.* I had fallen into this wickedness too, but your right hand upheld me, took me out of it, and placed me where I might recover. For you have said to man, *Behold, the fear of the Lord is wisdom,* and *Desire not to seem wise;* because they *who affirmed themselves to be wise, became fools.* And I had now found that pearl of great price, and I ought to have sold all that I had and bought it. But I hesitated.

2

So I WENT TO Simplicianus who, in the matter of receiving grace, had been the father of Ambrose, now bishop, and indeed Ambrose loved him as a father. I described to him the winding paths of my error. But when I told him that I had read some books of the Platonists which had been translated into Latin by Victorinus— once professor of rhetoric at Rome, who, so I had heard, had died a Christian—he congratulated me for not having fallen upon the writings of other philosophers full of *fallacies and deceits, after the rudiments of this world,* whereas in the Platonists God and His Word are everywhere implied. Then, in order to lead me toward the humility of Christ (*hidden from the wise, and revealed to little ones*), he went on to speak of Victorinus himself, with whom he had been on very friendly terms when he was in Rome. I shall make no secret of what he told me about him, for it is a story which ought to be confessed to you, containing, as it does, great praise of your grace. For Victorinus was an extremely learned old man, an expert scholar in all the liberal sciences, one who had read and weighed very many of the works of the philosophers, one who had been the teacher of numbers of distinguished senators and who, because of the exceptional brilliance of his teaching, had earned and accepted the honor of hav-

ing his statue set up in the Roman forum, a thing which
the citizens of this world regard as something quite remarkable, and up to old age he worshiped idols and took
part in those sacrilegious ceremonies which were the craze
with nearly all the Roman nobility, who had inspired the
people with their enthusiasm for Osiris and

> The dog Anubis and that monstrous brood
> Of deity which once took arms and fought
> In arms against Minerva, Neptune, Venus

—gods which Rome had conquered and to which she
now prayed, and for all these years old Victorinus, with
his thundering eloquence, had been the champion of
these gods; yet he did not blush to become the child of
your Christ, an infant at your font, bending his neck to
the yoke of humility and submitting his forehead to the
ignominy of the Cross.

O Lord, Lord, *Which has bowed the heavens and come
down, touched the mountains and they did smoke,* by
what means did you find your way into that man's heart?
According to Simplicianus, he read the Holy Scripture
and examined all Christian literature with the most
thorough and exact attention. He then said to Simplicianus
—not in public, but in a private friendly conversation—
"I should like you to know that I am now a Christian."
Simplicianus replied: "That I will not believe, and I shall
not count you as a Christian until I see you in the Church
of Christ." Victorinus smiled and said: "Is it the walls,
then, that make Christians?" And he often repeated that
he was a Christian, and Simplicianus often made the same
reply which was again countered by the joke about the
walls. For Victorinus was afraid of offending his friends,

who were important people and worshipers of these devils; he feared a great torrent of ill will falling upon him from the height of their Babylonian dignity, as from the tops of the cedars of Lebanon which the Lord had not yet brought down. But from his reading and deep meditation he drew strength. He feared that, if he was afraid to confess Christ before men, Christ might deny him in front of the holy angels, and it seemed to him that he was guilty of a great crime in being ashamed of the sacraments of the humility of your Word, while not being ashamed of the sacrilegious rites of those proud demons, in which he, imitating their pride, had taken part. So he turned his pride against what was vain, and kept his humility for the truth. Quite suddenly and unexpectedly he said to Simplicianus, as Simplicianus himself told me, "Let us go to the Church. I want to be made a Christian." And Simplicianus, who could not contain himself for joy, went along with him. Soon after he had received instruction in the first mysteries, he gave in his name as one who wished to be regenerated by baptism. Rome wondered and the Church rejoiced. The proud *saw and were wroth; they gnashed with their teeth and melted away*. But the Lord God was the hope of your servant, and *he regarded not vanities and lying* madness.

Finally the time came for him to make his profession of faith. At Rome this was usually done by those who were about to enter into your grace, and there was a fixed form of words which was learned by heart and spoken from a platform in the sight of the faithful. In the case of Victorinus, however, so Simplicianus told me, the priests gave him the opportunity to make his profession in a less public manner—as was often allowed to those who seemed likely to be frightened or embarrassed by the ceremony. But

Victorinus preferred to declare openly his salvation in front of the holy congregation. In the past he had taught rhetoric and there had been no salvation in that; yet he had publicly professed it. He had shown no nervousness when using his own words in front of crowds of people who could scarcely be described as sane; why, then, in front of your meek flock, should he fear to pronounce your Word? So, when he mounted the platform to make his profession, all those who knew him (and who was there who did not?) began to whisper his name one to another in glad murmurs. From the lips of the whole rejoicing people came the soft sound: "Victorinus, Victorinus." Quickly the sound had arisen because of the exultation they felt when they saw him, and now quickly they became silent again so as to hear him speak. With a fine confidence he declared openly the true faith, and they all wished that they could draw him into their very hearts. And in their love and their rejoicing (for these were the hands they used) they did take him into their hearts.

3

O GOOD GOD, what is it in men that makes them rejoice more when a soul that has been despaired of and is in very great danger is saved than when there has always been hope and the danger has not been so serious? For you too, merciful father, dost *more rejoice over one penitent than over ninety-nine just persons, that need no repentance.* We too are filled with joy whenever we hear the story of how the sheep which had strayed was brought back on the exultant shoulders of the shepherd and of how the coin was put back into your treasury with all the neighbors of the woman who found it rejoicing.

And the joy we feel in the solemn service of your house brings tears to our eyes, when in your house we hear read the story of your *younger son, that he was dead and lived again; had been lost and is found.* Indeed you rejoice in us and you rejoice in your angels who are holy in holy charity. For you are always the same, and as to those things which do not always exist or do not always exist in the same way, you know all of them, always and in the same way.

What is it in the soul, then, which makes it take more pleasure in the finding or recovery of things it loves than in the continual possession of them? There are all sorts of other examples of this; indeed the evidence is everywhere, simply crying out: "It is so." The victorious general has his triumph; but he would not have been victorious if he had not fought a battle, and the more danger there was in the battle, the more joy there is in the triumph. Sailors are tossed by a storm and in danger of shipwreck; they all grow pale at the thought of approaching death; then sky and sea become calm and their joy is just as excessive as was their fear. A friend is ill and his pulse shows that he is in danger; all who want him to be well become sick in mind with him; then he recovers, though he cannot walk yet quite as easily as he used to do; but there is already more joy than there was before, when he was well and perfectly able to walk. Also with regard to the ordinary pleasures of life, men seek them by way of difficulty and discomfort which are voluntary and self-chosen and not the kind which comes upon them unexpectedly and against their wills. There is no pleasure in eating or drinking unless it is preceded by the discomfort of being hungry or thirsty. Drunkards eat various kinds of salty things in order to produce an uncomfortable dryness, and, when this is alleviated by drink, they feel pleasure. It is also customary for girls who are engaged not to be given over immediately to their bridegrooms, the idea being that the husband may hold a woman cheap unless, while engaged, he has sighed for the long time he has had to wait.

We notice this, then, in pleasures that are foul and disgraceful and also in pleasures which are lawful and permitted; we notice it in the pure sincerity of friendship, and also in the case of him who was dead and became alive again, who had been lost and was found. Everywhere we find that the more pain there is first, the more joy there is after. Why is this, my Lord God? For you are to yourself eternal joy, you yourself are joy, and those beings who are around you find their joy forever in you. Why is it that this part of the universe alternates between deprivation and fulfillment, between discord and harmony? Or is this its condition, the measure given to it by you when, from the heights of heaven to the depths of earth, from the beginning to the end of time, from the angel to the worm, from the first movement to the last, you settled all the varieties of good and all your just works each in its proper place, each to be in its appointed time? I am abashed when I think how high you are in what is highest, how deep in what is deepest. Nowhere do you depart from us, and hard it is for us to return to you.

4

COME, LORD, act upon us and rouse us up and call us back! Fire us, clutch us, let your sweet fragrance grow upon us! Let us love, let us run! Certainly there are many who from a deeper hell of blindness than Victorinus come back to you and approach you and are enlightened with that light which *those who receive, receive power from Thee to become Thy sons*. But if they are not so well known in the world there is not so much rejoicing even among those who do know them; for when many people rejoice together, the joy of each individual is all the richer, since each one inflames the other and the warmth spreads throughout them all. Then too by the mere fact of being well known they have a great influence on others, leading them to salvation; they go first and many will follow in their steps. Thus even those who have gone before them on the same way feel great joy, and the joy is not only for them. Indeed we must certainly not think that in your tabernacle the persons of the rich should be more welcome than the poor, or the people of birth more welcome than the ordinary man. Since *Thou hast chosen the weak things of the world, to confound the strong, and the base things of this world, and the things despised hast Thou chosen, and those things which are not, that Thou mightest bring to nought things that are*. These words of yours were spoken by the tongue of *the least of your apostles*. Yet when, as the result of his good service, the pride of Paulus the proconsul was so beaten down that he came under the light yoke of your Christ and became a simple subject of the great king, the apostle, to mark the glory of such a victory, wished to be called Paul instead of Saul, as he was called previously. For the defeat of the enemy is all the more conspicuous when one wins over from him a man of whom he has a particular hold and through whom he can particularly influence others. And people of importance in the world satisfy both conditions; their nobility gives him a particular hold over them, and their authority enables him to use them as an in-

fluence over others. It was natural, therefore, for there to
be a particular welcome for the heart of Victorinus, which
the devil had held as an impregnable stronghold, and for
the tongue of Victorinus, which the devil had made use
of as a strong and keen weapon for the destruction of so
many. And it was right for your sons to feel a particular
joy because our King had bound the strong man, and they
saw his *vessels taken from him and cleansed,* and *made
meet for Thy honor, and become serviceable for the
Lord, unto every good work.*

5

WHEN THIS MAN of yours, Simplicianus, told me all
this about Victorinus, I was on fire to be like him,
and this, of course, was why he had told me the story. He
told me this too—that in the time of the Emperor Julian,
when a law was passed forbidding Christians to teach
literature and rhetoric, Victorinus had obeyed the law,
preferring to give up his talking-shop rather than your
Word, by which you make even the tongues of infants
eloquent. In this I thought that he was not only brave
but lucky, because he had got the chance of giving all
his time to you. This was just what I longed for myself,
but I was held back, and I was held back not by fetters
put on me by someone else, but by the iron bondage of
my own will. The enemy held my will and made a chain
out of it and bound me with it. From a perverse will
came lust, and slavery to lust became a habit, and the
habit, being constantly yielded to, became a necessity.
These were like links, hanging each to each (which is
why I called it a chain), and they held me fast in a hard
slavery. And the new will which I was beginning to have
and which urged me to worship you in freedom and to

enjoy you, God, the only certain joy, was not yet strong enough to overpower the old will which by its oldness had grown hard in me. So my two wills, one old, one new, one carnal, one spiritual, were in conflict, and they wasted my soul by their discord.

In this way my personal experience enabled me to understand what I had read—that *the flesh lusteth against the spirit and the spirit against the flesh.* I, no doubt, was on both sides, but I was more myself when I was on the side which I approved of for myself than when I was on the side of which I disapproved. For it was no longer really I myself who was on this second side, since there to a great extent I was rather suffering things against my will than doing them voluntarily. Yet it was my own fault that habit fought back so strongly against me; for I had come willingly where I now did not will to be. And who has any right to complain when just punishment overtakes the sinner? Nor did I have any longer the excuse which I used to think I had when I said that the reason why I had not yet forsaken the world and given myself up to your service was because I could not see the truth clearly. Now I could see it perfectly clearly. But I was still tied down to earth and refused to take my place in your army. And I was just as frightened of being freed from all my hampering baggage as I ought to have been frightened of being hampered. The pack of this world was a kind of pleasant weight upon me, as happens in sleep, and the thoughts in which I meditated on you were like the efforts of someone who tries to get up but is so overcome with drowsiness that he sinks back again into sleep. Of course no one wants to sleep forever, and everyone in his senses would agree that it is better to be awake; yet all the same, when we feel a sort of lethargy in our limbs, we often put off the moment of shaking off sleep, and, even though it is time to get up, we gladly take a little longer in bed, conscious though we may be that we should not be doing so. In just the same way I was quite certain that it was better to give myself up to your charity rather than to give in to my own desires; but, though the former course was a conviction to which I gave my assent, the latter was a pleasure to which I gave my consent. For I had no answer to make to you when you called me: *Awake, thou that sleepest, and arise from the dead, and Christ shall give thee light.* And, while you showed me wherever I looked that what you said was true, I, convinced by the truth, could still find nothing at all to say except lazy words spoken half asleep: "A minute," "just a minute," "just a little time longer." But there was no limit to the minutes, and the little time longer went a long way. It was in vain that *I delighted in Thy law according to the inner man, when another law in my members rebelled against the law of my mind, and led me captive under the law of sin which was in my members.* For the law of sin is the strong force of habit, which drags the mind along and controls it even against its will —though deservedly, since the habit was voluntarily adopted. *Who then should deliver me thus wretched from the body of this death, but Thy grace only, through Jesus Christ our Lord?*

6

Now, LORD, my helper and my redeemer, I shall tell and confess to your name how it was that you freed me from the bondage of my desire for sex, in which I was so closely fettered, and from my slavery to the affairs of this world. I was leading my usual life; my

anxiety was growing greater and greater, and every day
I sighed to you. I went often to your Church, whenever
I had time to spare from all that business under the
weight of which I was groaning. Alypius was with me.
He was free from his official legal work after a third term
as assessor and was now waiting to sell his legal advice
to anyone who came along, just as I was selling the ability
to make speeches—if such an ability can be imparted
by teaching. Nebridius, as an act of friendship to us, had
consented to teach under Verecundus, a great friend of
us all, a citizen and elementary schoolmaster of Milan.
He had been very eager to have Nebridius on his staff and
indeed had claimed it as something due from our
friendship that one of us should come and give him the
help and support which he badly needed. Nebridius was
not influenced by any desire for profit; he could have
done better for himself by teaching literature, if he had
wanted. But he was the kindest and best of friends,
and, being always ready to help others, would not turn
down our request. He conducted himself very carefully
in his work, being unwilling to become known in what
are regarded by the world as "distinguished circles," and
avoiding everything which could disturb his peace of
mind; for he wanted to have his mind free and at leisure
for as many hours as possible so as to pursue wisdom, to
read about it, or to hear about it.

One day, when Alypius and I were at home (Nebridius, for some reason which I cannot remember, was
away) we were visited by a man called Ponticianus who,
coming from Africa, was a fellow countryman of ours and
who held an important appointment at the emperor's
court. He had something or other which he wanted to ask
us, and we sat down to talk. In front of us was a table for

playing games on, and he happened to notice a book lying on the table. He took it, opened it, and found that it was the apostle Paul. He was quite surprised at this, since he had imagined it would be one of the books over which I wearied myself out in the course of my profession. Next he began to smile and, looking closely at me, told me that he was not only surprised but pleased at his unexpected discovery that I had this book and only this book at my side. For he was a Christian, and baptized. He often knelt before you, our God, in Church, praying long and frequently to you. I told him that I gave the greatest attention to these works of Scripture, and then, on his initiative, a conversation began about the Egyptian monk Antony, whose name was very well known among your servants, although Alypius and I up to this time had never heard of him. When Ponticianus discovered this he talked all the more about him, since he wanted us in our ignorance, at which he was much surprised, to learn more about such a great man. And we were amazed as we heard of these wonderful works of yours which had been witnessed by so many people, had been done in the true faith and the Catholic Church, and all so recently—indeed practically in our own times. All of us were full of wonder, Alypius and I at the importance of what we were hearing, Ponticianus at the fact that we had never heard the story before.

He went on to speak of the communities living in monasteries, of their way of life which was full of the sweet fragrance of you, and of the fruitful deserts in the wilderness, about which we knew nothing. There was actually a monastery in Milan outside the walls of the city. It was full of good brothers and was under the care of Ambrose, but we had not even heard of this. So

Ponticianus went on speaking and we sat quiet, listening to him eagerly. In the course of his talk he told us how once, when the emperor was at Treves and busy with holding the chariot races in the Circus, he himself with three friends had gone for a walk in the afternoon through the gardens near the city walls. It happened that they walked in two groups, one of the three going one way with him, and the others going another way by themselves. These other two, as they strolled along, happened to come to a small house which was inhabited by some of your servants, *poor in spirit, of whom is the kingdom of heaven,* and there they found a book in which was written an account of the life of Antony. One of the two friends began to read it. He became full of wonder and excitement, and, as he read, he began to think of how he himself could lead a life like this and, abandoning his profession in this world, give his service to you. For these two men were both officials in the emperor's civil service. Suddenly, then, he was filled with a holy love; he felt a sober shame, and, angry with himself, he looked toward his friend and said: "Tell me now; in all this hard work which we do, what are we aiming at? What is it that we want? Why is it that we are state officials? Can we have any higher hope at court than to become friends of the emperor? And is not that a position difficult to hold and full of danger? Indeed does one not have to go through danger after danger simply to reach a place that is more dangerous still? And how long will it take to get there? But, if I want, I can be the friend of God now, this moment." After saying this, he turned back to the book, troubled and perplexed by the new life to which he was giving birth. So he read on, and his heart, where you saw it, was changed, and, as soon appeared, his mind shook off the burden of the world. While he was reading and the waves in his heart rose and fell, there were times when he cried out against himself, and then he distinguished the better course and chose it for his own. Now he was yours, and he said to his friend: "I have now broken away from all our hopes and ambitions and have decided to serve God, and I am entering on this service now, this moment, in this place. You may not like to imitate me in this, but you must not oppose me."

The other replied that he would stay with him and be his comrade in so great a service and for so great a reward. Both of them were now yours; they were building their own fortress at the right cost—namely, the forsaking of all that they had and the following of you.

At this point Ponticianus and his companion, who had been walking in a different part of the garden, looking for their friends, came and found them in this place. When they found them, they suggested that they should go back, as it was now nearly sunset. The others however told them of the decision which they had reached and what they proposed to do; they described how the whole thing had started and how their resolution was now fixed, and they begged their friends, if they would not join them, not to interfere with their purpose. Ponticianus and his friend, while not changing from their former ways, did (as Ponticianus told us) weep for themselves and, devoutly and sincerely congratulating the others, asked them to remember them in their prayers; then, with their own hearts still down on the earth, they went off to the palace. But the other two, with their hearts fixed on heaven, remained there in the cottage. Each of these two was engaged to be married, and when the

girls to whom they were engaged heard what had happened, they also dedicated their virginity to you.

7

THIS WAS WHAT Ponticianus told us. But you, Lord,
while he was speaking, were turning me around so that
I could see myself; you took me from behind my own
back, which was where I had put myself during the time
when I did not want to be observed by myself, and you
set me in front of my own face so that I could see how foul
a sight I was—crooked, filthy, spotted, and ulcerous. I
saw and I was horrified, and I had nowhere to go to
escape from myself. If I tried to look away from myself,
Ponticianus still went on with his story, and again you
were setting me in front of myself, forcing me to look
into my own face, so that I might see my sin and hate
it. I did know it, but I pretended that I did not. I had
been pushing the whole idea away from me and for-
getting it.

But now the more ardent was the love I felt for those
two men of whom I was hearing and of how healthfully
they had been moved to give themselves up entirely to
you to be cured, the more bitter was the hatred I felt
for myself when I compared myself with them. Many
years (at least twelve) of my own life had gone by since
the time when I was nineteen and was reading Cicero's
Hortensius and had been fired with an enthusiasm for
wisdom. Yet I was still putting off the moment when,
despising this world's happiness, I should give all my
time to the search for that of which not only the finding
but merely the seeking must be preferred to the discovered treasures and kingdoms of men or to all the

pleasures of the body easily and abundantly available. But I, wretched young man that I was—even more wretched at the beginning of my youth—had begged you for chastity and had said: "Make me chaste and continent, but not yet." I was afraid that you might hear me too soon and cure me too soon from the disease of a lust which I preferred to be satisfied rather than extinguished. And I had gone along evil ways, following a sacrilegious superstition—not because I was convinced by it, but simply preferring it to the other doctrines into which I never inquired in a religious spirit, but merely attacked them in a spirit of spite.

I had thought that the reason why I was putting off from day to day the time when I should despise all worldly hopes and follow you alone was because I could see no certainty toward which I could direct my course. But now the day had come when in my own eyes I was stripped naked and my conscience cried out against me: "Can you not hear me? Was it not this that you used to say, that you would not throw off the burden of vanity for a truth that was uncertain? Well, look. Now the truth is certain, and you are still weighed down by your burden. Yet these others, who have not been so worn out in the search and not been meditating the matter for ten years or more, have had the weight taken from their backs and have been given wings to fly."

So I was being gnawed at inside, and as Ponticianus went on with his story I was lost and overwhelmed in a terrible kind of shame. When the story was over and the business about which he had come had been settled he went away, and I retired into myself. Nor did I leave anything unsaid against myself. With every scourge of condemnation I lashed my soul on to follow me now that

I was trying to follow you. And my soul hung back; it refused to follow, and it could give no excuse for its refusal. All the arguments had been used already and had been shown to be false. There remained a mute shrinking; for it feared like death to be restrained from the flux of a habit by which it was melting away into death.

8

AND NOW inside my house great indeed was the quarrel which I had started with my soul in that bedroom of my heart which we shared together. My looks were as disordered as my mind as I turned on Alypius and cried out to him: "What is wrong with us? What is this which you have just heard? The unlearned rise up and *take heaven by force,* while we (look at us!) with all our learning are wallowing in flesh and blood. Is it because they have gone ahead that we are ashamed to follow? And do we feel no shame at not even following at all?" Some such words as these I spoke, and then the disturbance in my mind tore me away from him, while he stared at me in silence and amazed. For I sounded strange to him. My forehead, cheeks, eyes, color of face, and inflection of voice expressed my mind better than the words I used.

There was a garden attached to our lodging, and we had the use of this as of the whole house; for our landlord, the owner of the house, did not live there. To this garden the tumult in my heart had driven me, as to a place where no one could intervene in this passionate suit which I had brought against myself until it could be settled—though how it would be settled you knew, not I. As to me I was mad and dying; but there was sanity in my madness, life in my death; I knew how evil I was; I did not know how well I would be soon.

So I withdrew to the garden and Alypius followed close after me. When he was there, I still felt myself in privacy, and how could he leave me when I was in such a state? We sat down as far as possible from the house. My spirit was in a turmoil; I was boiling with indignation against myself for not entering into your will and covenant, my God, where all my bones cried out that I should enter and praised it to the skies. And the way there is not by ship or chariot or on foot; the distance is not so great as that which I had come from the house to the place where we were sitting. All I had to do was to will to go there, and I would not only go but would immediately arrive; but it was necessary for the will to be resolute and sincere, not the turning and twisting this way and that of a will that was half maimed, struggling, with one part rising and another part falling.

Then in the middle of this storm of mental hesitation I made many movements with my body—the kind of movements which people sometimes want to make, but cannot make, either because they have not the limbs, or because their limbs are bound or weakened by illness or in some way or other prevented from action. But I, if I tore my hair, beat my forehead, locked my fingers together, clasped my knee, was performing these actions because I willed to do so. But I might have willed to do so and still not done so if the power of motion in my limbs had not followed the dictates of my will. So I was performing all sorts of actions where the will to do and the power to do are not the same thing, and I was not doing something the idea of which pleased me incomparably more and which soon after, when I should have the will, I should have the power to do, since when I willed, I should will it thoroughly. For in this matter the power was the same thing as the will, and merely to will was already to perform. And yet this was not done. It was easier for my body to obey the slightest intimation of the soul's will that the limbs should be put immediately in motion than it was for the soul to give obedience to itself so as to carry out by the mere act of willing what was its own great will.

9

WHAT CAN BE the explanation of such an absurdity? Enlighten me with your mercy, so that I may ask the question, if perhaps an answer may be found in the secret places of man's punishment and in those darkest agonies of the sons of Adam. What can be the explanation of such an absurdity? The mind gives an order to the body, and the order is obeyed immediately: the mind gives an order to itself, and there is resistance. The mind orders the hand to move, and such readiness is shown that you can hardly distinguish the command from its execution. Yet the mind is mind, and the hand is body. The mind orders the mind to will; it is the same mind, yet it does not obey. What can be the explanation of such an absurdity? The mind, I say, orders itself to will: it would not give the order, unless it willed it, yet it does not obey the order. The fact is that it does not will the thing entirely; consequently it does not give the order entirely. The force of the order is in the force of the will, and disobedience to the order results from insufficiency of the will. For the will orders that there should be a will—not a different will, but itself. But it is not entire in itself when it gives the order, and therefore its order is not obeyed. For if it were entire in itself, it would not give the order to will; the will would be there already. So it is not an absurdity partly to will and partly not to will; it is rather a sickness of the soul which is weighed down with habit so that it cannot rise up in its entirety, lifted aloft by truth. So the reason why there are two wills in us is because one of them is not entire, and one has what the other lacks.

10

LET THEM PERISH from your presence, God, as perish empty talkers and seducers of the soul, who, having observed that there are two wills in the act of deliberating, conclude from this that we have in us two minds of two different natures, one good and one evil. They themselves are truly evil, when they hold these evil opinions, and they are just as capable of becoming good if they will realize the truth and agree with the truth, so that your apostle may say to them: *Ye were sometimes darkness, but now light in the Lord.* But these people, by imagining that the nature of the soul is what God is, want to be light, not in the Lord, but in themselves, and the result is that they have become an even deeper darkness, since in their appalling arrogance they have gone further away from you—from you, *the true Light that enlighteneth every man that cometh into the world.* Take heed what you say, and blush for shame: *draw near unto Him and be enlightened, and your faces shall not be ashamed.*

As to me, when I was deliberating about entering the service of the Lord my God, as I had long intended to do, it was I who willed it, and it was I who was unwilling. It was the same "I" throughout. But neither my will nor my unwillingness was whole and entire. So I fought with myself and was torn apart by myself. It was against my will that this tearing apart took place, but this was not an indication that I had another mind of a different nature; it was simply the punishment which I was suffering in my own mind. It was not I, therefore, who caused it, but *the sin dwells in me,* and, being a son of Adam, I was suffering for his sin which was more freely committed.

For if there are as many contrary natures as there are conflicting wills, we shall find that there are not two only, but many more. Suppose a man is wondering whether to go to one of the Manichaean conventicles or to the theater; the Manichees will say: "Here is an example of the two natures, one good, leading in one direction, one bad, leading in another. How else can you explain the hesitation caused by two wills in opposition to each other?" But I should say that both wills are bad— the one that takes a man to the Manichees and the one which takes him to the theater instead. But they of course believe that the will which takes a man to them must necessarily be good. Very well, then. Suppose now the case of one of us who, also with two wills struggling inside him, is wondering whether to go to the theater or to our Church. Will not the Manichees also be in a state of indecision about what to say on this point? They will either have to make an admission which they would be most reluctant to make—namely, that it is a good will which takes a man to our Church, just as the will is good which leads men who have received and are bound by their sacraments to their church; or else they will have to assume that in one man there are two evil natures and two evil wills in conflict, and then what they are always

saying will not be true—that there is one evil and one
good will. Otherwise they will have to be converted to
the truth and not deny that when one is making up one's
mind there is just one soul which is pulled in different
directions by different wills.

Therefore, they can no longer say, when they observe
two conflicting wills in one man, that the conflict is between two opposing minds, of two opposing substances,
from two opposing principles—one good, one evil. Their
arguments are checked, overthrown, and put out of court
by you, God of truth. Take the case, for example, when
both wills are bad, as when a man deliberates whether
to commit a murder by poison or by a dagger; whether
to seize this or that part of another man's property, since
he cannot seize both; whether to squander his money on
pleasure or to hoard it up like a miser; whether to go
to the races or to the theater, if they happen both to be
on the same day; or, as a third possibility, this same man
may be wondering whether to commit a theft from someone else's house, if he gets the chance; or, as a fourth
possibility, whether to commit adultery, supposing that
the opportunity occurs at the same time. Now if all these
four possibilities become practicable at the same moment
and all are equally desired, though they cannot all be done
simultaneously, the mind will be torn apart by four conflicting wills; indeed, considering the multitude of things
which can be desired, there may be even more than four
wills in conflict. But the Manichees do not hold that
there is a similar abundance of different substances.

The same principle holds with regard to wills that are
good. Let me ask them this question: Is it good to take
pleasure in reading the Apostle, and also good to take
pleasure in a sober psalm, and also good to discuss the

Gospel? In each case they will reply: "It is good." If then all these activities at one and the same time offer us equal pleasure, must it not be that different wills are pulling at a man's heart while he makes up his mind which activity in particular he should choose? All these wills are good, yet they conflict with one another until one particular choice has been made, toward which the whole will, which was previously divided, now turns entirely. So too when eternity offers us a higher pleasure and the delight in some temporal good holds us down below, it is the same soul which feels both impulses; only its will for one or the other course is not total and complete, and consequently it is torn apart and heavily distressed as truth puts one way first and habit will not allow the other way to be abandoned.

11

So I was sick and in torture. I reproached myself much more bitterly than ever, and I turned and twisted in my chain till I could break quite free. Only a little of it still held me, but it did still hold me. And you, Lord, in the secret places of my soul, stood above me in the severity of your mercy, redoubling the lashes of fear and shame, so that I should not give way once more and so that that small weak piece of chain which still remained should not instead of snapping grow strong again and tie me down more firmly than before. I was saying inside myself: "Now, now, let it be now!" and as I spoke the words I was already beginning to go in the direction I wanted to go. I nearly managed it, but I did not quite manage it. Yet I did not slip right back to the beginning; I was a stage above that, and I stood there to regain my breath. And I tried again and I was very nearly there;

I was almost touching it and grasping it, and then I was not there, I was not touching it, I was not grasping it; I hesitated to die to death and to live to life; inveterate evil had more power over me than the novelty of good, and as that very moment of time in which I was to become something else drew nearer and nearer, it struck me with more and more horror. But I was not struck right back or turned aside; I was just held in suspense.

Toys and trifles, utter vanities had been my mistresses, and now they were holding me back, pulling me by the garment of my flesh and softly murmuring in my ear: "Are you getting rid of us?" and "From this moment shall we never be with you again for all eternity?" and "From this moment will you never for all eternity be allowed to do this or to do that?" My God, what was it, what was it that they suggested in those words "this" or "that" which I have just written? I pray you in your mercy to keep such things from the soul of your servant. How filthy, how shameful were these things they were suggesting! And now their voices were not half so loud in my ears; now they no longer came out boldly to contradict me face to face; it was more as though they were muttering behind my back, stealthily pulling at my sleeve as I was going away so that I should turn and look at them. Yet still they did hold me back as I hesitated to tear myself away and to shake them off and to take the great step in the direction where I was called. Violence of habit spoke the words: "Do you think that you can live without them?"

But by now it spoke very faintly. In the direction toward which I had turned my face and still trembled to take the last step, I could see the chaste dignity of Continence; she was calm and serene, cheerful without wantonness, and it was in truth and honor that she was enticing me to come to her without hesitation, stretching out to receive and to embrace me with those holy hands of hers, full of such multitudes of good examples. With her were so many boys and girls, so much of youth, so much of every age, grave widows and women grown old in virginity, and in them all was Continence herself, not barren, but *a fruitful mother of children,* her joys, by you, Lord, her husband. She smiled at me and there was encouragement in her smile, as though she were saying: "Can you not do what these men and these women have done? Or do you think that their ability is in themselves and not in the Lord their God? It was the Lord God who gave me to them. Why do you try and stand by yourself, and so not stand at all? Let him support you. Do not be afraid. He will not draw away and let you fall. Put yourself fearlessly in His hands. He will receive you and will make you well."

And I was blushing for shame, because I could still hear the dim voices of those vanities, and still I hung back in hesitation. And again she seemed to be speaking: "Stop your ears against those unclean members of yours, so that they may be mortified. They tell you of delights, but not of such delights as the law of the Lord your God tells."

So went the controversy in my heart—about self, and self against self. And Alypius stayed close by me, waiting silently to see how this strange agitation of mine would end.

12

AND NOW FROM my hidden depths my searching thought had dragged up and set before the sight of my heart the whole mass of my misery. Then a huge storm rose up within me bringing with it a huge downpour of tears. So that I might pour out all these tears and speak the words that came with them I rose up from Alypius (solitude seemed better for the business of weeping) and went further away so that I might not be embarrassed even by his presence. This was how I felt and he realized it. No doubt I had said something or other, and he could feel the weight of my tears in the sound of my voice. And so I rose to my feet, and he, in a state of utter amazement, remained in the place where we had been sitting. I flung myself down on the ground somehow under a fig tree and gave free rein to my tears; they streamed and flooded from my eyes, an *acceptable sacrifice to Thee*. And I kept saying to you, not perhaps in these words, but with this sense: *"And Thou, O Lord, how long? How long, Lord; wilt Thou be angry forever? Remember not our former iniquities."* For I felt that it was these which were holding me fast. And in my misery I would exclaim: "How long, how long this 'tomorrow and tomorrow'? Why not now? Why not finish this very hour with my uncleanness?"

So I spoke, weeping in the bitter contrition of my heart. Suddenly a voice reaches my ears from a nearby house. It is the voice of a boy or a girl (I don't know which) and in a kind of singsong the words are constantly repeated: "Take it and read it. Take it and read it." At once my face changed, and I began to think carefully of whether the singing of words like these came into any kind of game which children play, and I could not remember that I had ever heard anything like it before. I checked the force of my tears and rose to my feet, being quite certain that I must interpret this as a divine command to me to open the book and read the first passage which I should come upon. For I had heard this about Antony: he had happened to come in when the Gospel was being read, and as though the words read were spoken directly to himself, had received the admonition: *Go, sell all that thou hast, and give to the poor, and thou shalt have treasure in heaven, and come and follow me.* And by such an oracle he had been immediately converted to you.

So I went eagerly back to the place where Alypius was sitting, since it was there that I had left the book of the Apostle when I rose to my feet. I snatched up the book, opened it, and read in silence the passage upon which my eyes first fell: *Not in rioting and drunkenness, not in chambering and wantonness, not in strife and envying: but put ye on the Lord Jesus Christ, and make not provision for the flesh in concupiscence.* I had no wish to read further; there was no need to. For immediately I had reached the end of this sentence it was as though my heart was filled with a light of confidence and all the shadows of my doubt were swept away.

Before shutting the book I put my finger or some other marker in the place and told Alypius what had happened. By now my face was perfectly calm. And Alypius in his turn told me what had been going on in himself, and which I knew nothing about. He asked to see the passage which I had read. I showed him and he went on further than the part I had read, nor did I know the words which followed. They were these: *Him that is weak in the faith, receive.* He applied this to himself and told me so. He was strengthened by the admonition; calmly and unhesitatingly he joined me in a purpose and a resolution so good, and so right for his character, which had always been very much better than mine.

The next thing we do is to go inside and tell my mother. How happy she is! We describe to her how it all took place, and there is no limit to her joy and triumph. Now she was praising you, *Who art able to do above that which we ask or think;* for she saw that with regard to me you had given her so much more than she used to ask for when she wept so pitifully before you. For you converted me to you in such a way that I no longer sought a wife nor any other worldly hope. I was now standing on that rule of faith, just as you had shown me to her in a vision so many years before. And so you had changed her mourning into joy, a joy much richer than she had desired and much dearer and purer than that which she looked for by having grandchildren of my flesh.

BOOK X

1

LET ME KNOW YOU, my known; *let me know Thee even as I am known.* Power of my soul, enter into it and fit it for yourself, so that you may have and hold it *without spot or wrinkle.* This is my hope, *therefore do I speak,* and in this hope is my joy, when my joy is healthy. As to the other things of this life, the more we weep for them the less they ought to be wept for, and the less we weep for them the more we ought to weep. For, see, you love the truth, and he that *doth the truth, cometh to the light.* This is what I want to do in my heart, in front of you, in my confession, and in my writing before many witnesses.

2

INDEED, LORD, to your eyes the very depths of man's conscience are exposed, and there is nothing in me that I could keep secret from you, even if I did not want to confess it. I should not be hiding myself from you, but you from myself. But now when my groaning bears evidence that I am displeased with myself, you shine out on me and are pleasing and loved and longed for, so that I am ashamed of myself and renounce myself and choose you and, except in you, can please neither you nor myself. Whatever I am, then, Lord, is open and evident to you. And what profit I have from confessing to you, I have already said. And I do not make my confession by means of the words and sounds of the flesh, but with the words of the soul and the crying out of my thought which your ear knows. For when I am wicked, confes-

137

sion to you is the same thing as being displeased with myself; when I am good, confession to you is the same thing as not attributing my goodness to myself. Since Thou, Lord, *blessest the godly,* but first *Thou justifieth him when ungodly.* So, my God, my confession in your sight is made to you both silently and not silently; there is no sound of words, but there is a clamor of feeling. For if I say anything good to men, you have heard it from me first, and if you hear any good from me, it was you who first told it to me.

3

WHY THEN DO I bother to let men hear my confessions? It is not as though men are likely *to heal all my infirmities.* Men are a race very inquisitive about other people's lives, very lazy in improving their own. Why should they want to hear from me what I am, when they do not want to hear from you what they are? And when they hear my own account of my own self, how do they know that I am telling the truth, seeing that *no man knows what is in man, but the spirit of man which is in him?* But if they hear from you something about their own selves they cannot say: "the Lord is lying." For to hear from you about themselves is simply to know themselves. And if one knows oneself and then says: "it is false," one must be lying oneself. But *charity believeth all things* (that is, among those whom it binds together and makes one), and so, Lord, I make my confession to you in such a way that men may hear it, though I cannot demonstrate to them that I am telling the truth; yet those whose ears are opened to me by charity believe what I say.

Yet still, my inmost Physician, I beg you to make clear

to me what advantage I get from doing this. You have forgiven and covered up my past sins, blessing me in you and changing my soul by faith and by your sacrament; yet when the confessions of these past sins are read and heard, they rouse up the heart and prevent it from sinking into the sleep of despair and saying "I cannot." Instead they encourage it to be wakeful in the love of your mercy and the sweetness of your grace, through which the weak is made strong when, thanks to this grace of yours, he becomes conscious of his own weakness. Also good men are pleased when they hear of sins done in the past by people who are now free from them; they are pleased not because of the sins themselves, but because what were sins have now ceased to exist.

But, my Lord, to whom every day my conscience makes its confession, more secure in the hope of your mercy than in its own innocence, tell me, I beg you, of what advantage it is when, in front of you, I also by means of this book confess to men not what I once was, but what I now am. As to my confession of the past, I have already seen and mentioned the advantages of that. But as to what I now am, at the very moment of writing these confessions, there are many people who want to know about this—both those who know me personally and those who do not, but have heard something about me or from me; but their ear is not laid against my heart, where I am whatever I am. And so they want, as I make my confession, to hear what I am inside myself, beyond the possible reach of their eyes and ears and minds. And in wanting to hear, they are ready to believe; but will they know? For that charity, by which they are good, tells them that I am not lying about myself in my confessions, and it is the charity in them that believes me.

4

BUT WHAT ADVANTAGE do they wish to gain from
this? Do they desire to rejoice with me when they hear
how close I have come to you by your grace? And to
pray for me, when they hear how I am kept back by
my own weight? It is to people like this that I shall
show myself. For it is no small advantage, my Lord God,
that many people should give thanks to you for me and
that many people should pray to you for me. I would
wish that their brotherly minds should love in me what
you teach them is to be loved, and should lament in me
what you teach them is to be lamented. It is a brotherly
mind that I would wish for, not the mind of strangers, not
that of the *strange children, whose mouth talketh of
vanity, and their right hand is a right hand of iniquity;*
but that brotherly mind which is glad for me when it
sees good in me and sorry for me when it sees bad in me,
because, whether it sees good or bad, it loves me. It is to
people like this that I shall show myself, hoping that in
my good deeds they will be glad and in my evil deeds they
will be sad. My good deeds are your work and your gift,
my evil deeds are my faults and your punishments. So I
would wish there to be gladness for the one, sadness for
the other, and that hymns and lamentations should rise
up into your sight from those censers which are the hearts
of my brethren. And I pray that you, Lord, pleased with
the sweet incense of your holy temple, may *have mercy
upon me according to Thy great mercy for Thine own
name's sake,* and, in no way forsaking what you have
begun, perfect my imperfections.

So in confessing not only what I have been but what
I am the advantage is this: I make my confession not

only in front of you, in a secret *exultation with trembling,* with a secret sorrow and with hope, but also in the ears of the believing sons of men, companions in my joy and sharers in my mortality, my fellow citizens and fellow pilgrims—those who have gone before and those who follow after and those who are on the road with me. These are your servants and my brothers; those whom you have willed to be your sons, my masters whom I am to serve if I wish to live with you and of you. And this word of yours to me would be a little thing if it only gave me a spoken command and did not also go in front of me in action. And so I do it both in deed and in word; I do it under your wings, and the danger would be too great if under your wings my soul were not subdued to you and my weakness known to you. I am only a little child, but my Father lives forever and my Protector is sufficient for me. For he is the same who begot me and who watches over me, and you yourself are all my good, you Almighty, who are with me even before I am with you. So it is to people like this, those whom you command me to serve, that I shall show not what I was, but what I now am and continue to be. *But neither do I judge myself.* It is in this way that I should like to be heard.

5

FOR *Thou, Lord, dost judge me;* because, although *no man knoweth the things of a man, but the spirit of a man which is in him,* yet there is still something of man which even the spirit of man that is in him does not know. But you, Lord, know all of him, you who made him. And as to me, though in your sight I despise myself and consider myself dust and ashes, yet still I know something of you which I do not know of myself. Cer-

tainly now we see through a glass darkly, and not yet *face to face,* and so, as long as I am on pilgrimage away from you, I am more present to myself than to you; yet I know that you are not in any way subject to violence, whereas I do not know in my case what temptations I can and what I cannot resist. And there is hope, because *Thou art faithful, Who wilt not suffer us to be tempted above that we are able; but wilt with the temptation also make a way to escape, that we may be able to bear it.* So I will confess what I know of myself, and I will also confess what I do not know of myself; because what I know of myself I know by means of your light shining upon me, and what I do not know remains unknown to me until *my darkness be made as the noonday* in your countenance.

6

THERE IS NO DOUBT in my mind, Lord, that I love you. I feel it with certainty. You struck my heart with your word, and I loved you. But, see, *heaven and earth and all that therein is* on every side are telling me to love you, and they never stop saying it to all men, *that they may be without excuse.* But more deeply *wilt Thou have mercy on whom Thou wilt have mercy, and wilt have compassion on whom Thou hast had compassion;* otherwise heaven and earth are telling your praises to deaf ears.

But what do I love when I love you? Not the beauty of the body nor the glory of time, not the brightness of light shining so friendly to the eye, not the sweet and various melodies of singing, not the fragrance of flowers and unguents and spices, not manna and honey, not limbs welcome to the embraces of the flesh: it is not these that I love when I love my God. And yet I do love a kind of light, melody, fragrance, food, embracement when I love my God; for He is the light, the melody, the fragrance, the food, the embracement of my inner self—there where is a brilliance that space cannot contain, a sound that time cannot carry away, a perfume that no breeze disperses, a taste undiminished by eating, a clinging together that no satiety will sunder. This is what I love when I love my God.

And what is this God? I asked the earth and it answered: "I am not he," and all things that are on the earth confessed the same. I asked the sea and the deeps and the creeping things with living souls, and they replied: "We are not your God. Look above us." I asked the blowing breezes, and the universal air with all its inhabitants answered: "Anaximenes was wrong. I am not God." I asked the heaven, the sun, the moon, the stars, and "No," they said, "we are not the God for whom you are looking." And I said to all those things which stand about the gates of my senses: "Tell me about my God, you who are not He. Tell me something about Him." And they cried out in a loud voice: "He made us." My question was in my contemplation of them, and their answer was in their beauty. And I turned my attention on myself and said to myself: "And you, who are you?" And I replied: "A man." Now I find evidently in myself a body and a soul, the one exterior, the other interior. Which of these should I have employed in seeking for my God? I had already looked for Him by means of the body, searching from earth to heaven, as far as I could send the beams of my eyes as messengers. But the interior part of me is the better. It was to this part that all the messengers from my body gave in their reports and this part sat in judgment weighing the replies of heaven and earth and all things within them when they said: "We are not

God," and when they said: "He made us." The inner
man knew these things by means of the ministry of the
outer man. I, the inner man, knew them, I, the soul, knew
them through the senses of my body. I asked the whole
mass and frame of the universe about my God, and it replied: "I am not he, but He made me."

Is not this appearance of the universe evident to all
whose senses are not deranged? Then why does it not
give the same answer to all? Animals, small and great, see
it, but cannot ask the question. They are not gifted with
reason to sit in judgment on the evidence brought in by
the senses. But men can ask the question, so that *the invisible things of God are clearly seen, being understood
by the things that are made;* but by loving these things,
they become subject to them, and subjects cannot judge.
And these things will only answer the questions of those
who are prepared to judge. Not that they alter their
speech—that is, their appearance. If one man merely
looks at them and another not only looks but asks his
question, they do not appear one thing to one man, and a
different thing to the other. They look just the same to
both, but to one man they say nothing and to the other
they speak. Or it would be truer to say that they speak to
everyone, but are only understood by those who compare
the voice which comes to them from outside with the
truth that is within. For truth says to me: "Your God is
not heaven or earth or any other body." Their very nature
declared this. Obviously there is less bulk in a part than
in the whole. And now, my soul, I say to you that you
are my better part; you animate the whole bulk of the
body, giving it life—a thing which no body can do for
another body. But your God is for you too the life of
your life.

7

WHAT, THEN, do I love when I love God? Who is
He that is above the summit of my soul? It is by my
soul herself that I shall ascend to Him. I shall go past
that force in me by which I cling to the body and fill its
frame with life. It is not by that force that I can find my
God; if it were so, the *horse and mule that have no understanding* might find Him, since their bodies too live
by this same force. But there is another force—not the
one by which I give life, but the one by which I give perception to my flesh. The Lord created this power in me,
commanding the eye not to hear and the ear not to see,
but giving me the eye to see by and the ear to hear by,
and so allotting to each of the other senses its own particular duty and function, and through these senses, with
all their diverse functions, I act, retaining my identity as
one soul. But I shall go past this force too; for the horse
and the mule have it too; they also perceive by means
of the body.

8

I SHALL PASS ON, then, beyond this faculty in my
nature as I ascend by degrees toward Him who made me.
And I come to the fields and spacious palaces of memory, where lie the treasures of innumerable images of all
kinds of things that have been brought in by the senses.
There too are our thoughts stored up, if by thought we
have increased or diminished or in any way altered
those things with which our senses have been in contact,
and there too is everything else that has been brought in
and deposited and has not yet been swallowed up and
buried in forgetfulness. When I am in this treasure house,

I ask for whatever I like to be brought out to me, and then some things are produced at once, some things take longer and have, as it were, to be fetched from a more remote part of the store, and some things come pouring out all together and, when in fact we want and are looking for something quite different, they thrust themselves forward as though they were saying: "Surely you must be looking for me." With the hand of my heart I brush them away from the face of my memory, until the thing that I want is discovered and brought out from its hidden place into my sight. And some things are produced easily and in perfect order, just as they are required; what comes first gives place to what comes next, and, as it gives place, it is stored up ready to be brought out when I need it again. All this happens when I repeat anything by heart.

Here are kept distinct and in their proper classifications all sensations which come to us, each by its own route: for instance, light, color, and the shapes of bodies reach us through the eyes; all kinds of sound through the ears; all smells by the nostrils; all tastes by the mouth, and by the sensation of the whole body we derive our impression of what is hard or soft, hot or cold, rough or smooth, heavy or light, whether from outside or inside the body itself. And the great harbor of memory, with its secret, numberless, and indefinable recesses, takes in all these things so that they may be reproduced and brought back again when the need arises. They all enter the memory by their various ways and are all stored up in the memory. Or rather it is not the things themselves that enter; what happens is that the images of things perceived are there ready at hand for thought to recall.

Precisely how these images are formed who can tell?

Though it is clear enough which sense was responsible for seizing hold of them and storing them up inside us. For even when I am surrounded by darkness and silence, I can, if I wish, summon up colors in my memory and tell the difference between black and white and any other colors I like, and while I am considering the images drawn in by my eyes, sounds do not come running in to disturb it, though they too are in my memory, stored up, as it were, in a separate compartment. For I can call for sounds also, if I wish, and they are present immediately; with no movement of tongue or vocal chords I sing as much as I like, and those images of color, which are still there in the memory, do not break in and interrupt when I call for something from that other storehouse which contains impressions brought in by the ear. In the same way I call up at pleasure all those other things which have been brought in and stored up by means of the other senses. I can tell the difference between the smell of lilies and of violets, though at the time I am smelling nothing; I prefer honey to sweet wine, something smooth to something rough, simply by memory and without using the sense either of taste or touch.

All this I do inside me, in the huge court of my memory. There I have by me the sky, the earth, the sea, and all things in them which I have been able to perceive— apart from what I have forgotten. There too I encounter myself; I recall myself—what I have done, when and where I did it, and in what state of mind I was at the time. There are all the things I remember to have experienced myself or to have heard from others. From the same store too I can take out pictures of things which have either happened to me or are believed on the basis of experience; I can myself weave them into the context of the past, and from them I can infer future actions, events, hopes, and then I can contemplate all these as though they were in the present. "I shall do this," or "I shall do that," I say to myself in this deep recess of my mind, full of the images of so many and of such great things, "and this or that follows." "Oh if only this or that could happen!" or "May God prevent this or that!" So I speak to myself, and, while I am speaking, the images of all the things that I am saying are present to my mind, all from this same treasury of my memory; indeed I would not be able to speak of these things at all if the images were not there.

How great, my God, is this force of memory, how exceedingly great! It is like a vast and boundless subterranean shrine. Who has ever reached the bottom of it? Yet this is a faculty of my mind and belongs to my nature; nor can I myself grasp all that I am. Therefore, the mind is not large enough to contain itself. But where can that uncontained part of it be? Is it outside itself and not inside? In that case, how can it fail to contain itself? At this thought great wonder comes over me; I am struck dumb with astonishment. And men go abroad to wonder at the heights of mountains, the huge waves of the sea, the broad streams of rivers, the vastness of the ocean, the turnings of the stars—and they do not notice themselves and they see nothing marvelous in the fact that when I was mentioning all these things I was not seeing them with my eyes, yet I would not have been able to speak of them unless these mountains and waves and rivers and stars (which I have seen) and the ocean (which I have heard about) had been visible to me inside, in my memory, and with just the same great spatial intervals and proportions as if I were really seeing them outside myself. Yet, when I saw them with my eyes, I did not by the act of seeing draw them into myself; it is not they but their images that are in me, and I know by what bodily sense each impression has come to me.

9

YET MORE STILL is contained in this immense capacity of my memory. Here too is everything that I have learned in the liberal sciences and not forgotten—removed somehow to an inner place, which is yet no place. And here I have with me not the images but the things themselves. What grammar is, or the art of disputation, or how many types of question there are—everything of this sort that I know is in my memory in a different way. Here it is not the case that I retain the image and leave the thing itself outside me. It is not the case of the sound of words which has ceased to sound, like a voice which has left a fixed impression on the ear by which it can be recalled as though it were sounding, when in fact it is not sounding; or like a smell which, while it is passing and vanishing into air, affects the sense of smell and so carries into the memory an image of itself which we can recall by the act of recollection; or like food, which certainly has no taste when it is in the stomach, but still has a kind of taste in our memory; or like something which is perceived by the sense of bodily touch and can still be imagined in our memory when it is no longer in contact with us. In all these cases it is not the things themselves that are brought into our memory; it is only their images which are seized upon with such amazing speed and are then, as it were, stored up in wonderful secret hiding places, from which by the act of remembering they can wonderfully be brought out again.

10

BUT WHEN I HEAR that there are three types of question—"Does the thing exist? What is it? Of what kind
is it?"—I certainly hold in my mind the images of the
sounds of which these words are compared, and I know
that they passed through the air, making a particular
kind of noise, and have now ceased to be. But as to the
things themselves that are signified by these sounds, I
never approached them by any bodily sense; my only
means of discerning them was through the mind, and in
my memory I have stored up, not their images, but the
things themselves. How they got into me, let them say if
they can. For as I go over all the gateways of my body,
I cannot find by which one they gained entrance. The
eyes say: "If these images were colored, it was we who
gave notice of them." The ears say: "If they made a
sound, it was by us that they were reported." The nostrils
say: "If they had a smell, they came in by way of us." And
the sense of taste says: "Unless one could taste them, it
is no use asking me." Touch says: "If the thing is not a
body I did not handle it, and if I did not handle it, I gave
no information about it." From where, then, and how
did they enter into my memory? I do not know. For when
I learned them, I was not taking them on trust from some
other mind; I was recognizing them in my own mind;
I accepted them as true and committed them to my mind
as though I were depositing them in some place where I
could find them again whenever I wanted. So they were
in my mind, even before I learned them, but they were
not in my memory. Then where were they? Or how was
it that, when I heard them spoken, I recognized them and
said: "That is right. That is true," unless in fact they were

in my memory already, but so far back and so buried, as it were, in the furthest recesses that, if they had not been dragged out by the suggestion of someone else, I should perhaps not have been able to conceive of them?

11

WE FIND, THEREFORE, that to learn those things which we do not draw into us as images by means of our senses, but which we perceive inside ourselves as they actually are without the aid of images means simply this: by the act of thought we are, as it were, collecting together things which the memory did contain, though in a disorganized and scattered way, and by giving them our close attention we are arranging for them to be as it were stored up ready to hand in that same memory where previously they lay hidden, neglected, and dispersed, so that now they will readily come forward to the mind that has become familiar with them. My memory carries a very great number of things of this sort, which have been discovered and, as I said, placed as it were ready to hand. These are the things which we are said to have learned and to know. Yet if I cease, even for quite a short space of time, to bring them up into my mind, down they sink again and slip away into some sort of distant hidden place, so that I have to think them out afresh from that same place (for there is nowhere else where they can have gone) and once again gather them together so that they may be known. In fact what one is doing is collecting them from their dispersal. Hence the derivation of the word "to cogitate." For *cogo* (collect) and *cogito* (recollect) are in the same relation to each other as *ago* and *agito, facio* and *factito*. But the mind has appropriated to itself this word ("cogitation"), so that it is only correct to say "cogitated" of things which are "re-collected" in the mind, not of things re-collected elsewhere.

12

THE MEMORY also contains the innumerable principles and laws of numbers and dimensions. None of these has been imprinted on it by any bodily sense, since none of these is colored or can be heard, smelled, tasted, or touched. I have heard the sounds of the words by which these principles are signified when we discuss them, but the sounds and the principle are different things. The sounds will be different if the words used are Greek or Latin, but the principles are neither Greek nor Latin nor any other language. I have seen the lines drawn by architects, lines barely visible, like spiders' webs. But the principles involved are something different; they are not images of those things which are reported to me by my bodily eye, and the man who knows these principles recognizes them inside him without having to think of any kind of material body. Again, with all my bodily senses I have perceived the numbers which we use in counting; but the numbers by which we are able to count at all are not the same as these, nor are they images of these; they have a real existence of their own. Anyone who cannot see them may laugh at me for talking of them, and, while he laughs, I shall be sorry for him.

13

ALL THESE THINGS I hold in my memory, and I also hold in my memory how I learned them. And there are many completely false arguments which I have heard advanced against these things; these also I hold in my

memory. And though they are false, it is not false to
say that I remember them. I also remember that I have
distinguished between the truths and the false objections
made to those truths. And I see that for me to make the
distinction between them now is a different thing from
remembering how I often did make the distinction in the
past, when I was thinking on these subjects. Therefore I
remember that I often did understand them and also I
store up in my memory what I see and understand now,
so that later I may remember what I did understand at
this moment. So I remember that I have remembered, and
if in the future I recall that I have now been able to remember these things, it will be by the force of my
memory that I shall recall it.

14

THIS SAME MEMORY also contains the feelings of my
mind. It does not contain them in the same way as the
mind itself has them when it is experiencing them, but in
a very different way, appropriate to the nature of memory.
For I remember that I was happy when I am not happy
now, and I recall my past sadness when I am not sad
now; when I am not frightened, I can remember that I
once was frightened, and I can recall a desire I had once,
when I have it no longer. Sometimes it works the other
way: when I am happy I remember my past sadness,
and when I am sad I remember my past happiness. There
is nothing surprising in this, so far as the body is concerned; for the mind is one thing and the body another.
So if I remember with joy some past pain of the body,
there is nothing strange in that. But memory itself is
mind. For example, when we tell someone to remember
something we say: "Be sure to keep it in mind," and

when we forget something we say: "It was not in my mind," or "It slipped out of my mind." So we call memory itself mind. Now since this is so, how is it that when I, being happy, remember my past sadness—so that the mind contains happiness and the memory contains sadness—the mind is happy because of the happiness in it, but the memory is not sad because of the sadness in it? Is it that the memory has no connection with the mind? Obviously one cannot say that. Therefore the memory must be, as it were, the stomach of the mind, and happiness and sadness like sweet and bitter food, and when they are committed to the memory it is as though they passed into the stomach where they can be stored up but cannot taste. A ridiculous comparison, perhaps, and yet there is some truth in it.

Observe too that it comes from my memory when I say that there are four types of disturbance in the mind—desire, joy, fear, sorrow—and in any statements that I may be able to make on these subjects by means of definition or classification under genus and species, it is in my memory that I find what to say and it is from my memory that I bring it out. Yet in calling back to mind by the act of recollection disturbances of this sort, I myself feel no disturbance, and they were there, in the memory, before I recalled them and brought them back; indeed it was only because they were there that I was able to recollect them. May one say, then, that just as food is brought up from the stomach by chewing the cud, so these things are brought up from the memory by recollection? But why then is the actual sweetness of joy or bitterness of sorrow not tasted in the cogitational mouth of the man who makes statements about, i.e., remembers, these things? Or is this the point where the comparison between rumination and recollection is incomplete? For we would be reluctant to talk about these subjects if, whenever we used the words "sorrow" or "fear," we had actually to feel sorrow or fear. Yet we could not talk about them at all, unless we could find within our memory not only the sounds of the words (according to images impressed upon it by the senses of the body) but also concepts of the things themselves, and we did not receive these concepts by the gateway of any bodily sense; it was the mind itself which, by the experience of its own passions, felt them and entrusted them to the memory; or else the memory retained them, even if they were not entrusted to it.

15

BUT IT IS NOT easy to say whether this takes place by means of images or not. I pronounce the word "stone" or "sun" when the things themselves are not present to my senses; images of them however are in front of my memory. I pronounce the word for some physical pain; this pain is not present to me, since I am not in pain; but unless the image of it was in my memory, I should not know how to speak of it and, in any discussion, I should be unable to draw a distinction between it and pleasure. I mention physical health, when I myself am in good health; the thing signified by the words is actually present in me, yet unless its image also was in my memory, it would be impossible for me to recall what is meant by the sound of the words denoting it; nor, when the word "health" was mentioned, would sick people recognize the meaning of what was said, unless, in spite of the fact that health itself was not in their bodies, they still retained through the force of memory an image of health. I name

the numbers that we use in counting; it is the numbers
themselves and not their images that are in my memory.
I name the image of the sun, and this image is in my
memory—not the image of its image, but the image itself; that is what is before me when I recall it. I say
"memory" and I recognize what I mean by it; but where
do I recognize it except in my memory itself? Can memory itself be present to itself by means of its image
rather than by its reality?

16

Now SUPPOSE I say "forgetfulness" and once again
recognize what I mean by the word, how do I recognize
the thing itself unless it were that I remembered it? I
am not speaking of the sound of the word, but the thing
which the word signifies; for if I had forgotten the thing,
I should certainly not be able to recognize what the
word meant. When I remember memory, memory itself
is, through itself, present to itself; but when I remember
forgetfulness, there are present both memory and forgetfulness—memory by which I remember, forgetfulness
which I remember. But what is forgetfulness except privation of memory? How then can it be present for me
to remember it, when I am not able to remember it
when it is present? But if we retain in our memory what
we remember, and if, unless we remembered forgetfulness, we should be quite unable to recognize what was
meant by the word when we heard it, then forgetfulness
must be retained in the memory. Therefore, what, when
present, we forget is present in order that we should not
forget. Must we understand from this that forgetfulness,
when we remember it, is not present to the memory in
itself, but by its image, because if it were present in it-

self, it would cause us, not to remember, but to forget? Who can possibly find the answer to this or understand how it comes about?

For me, Lord, certainly this is hard labor, hard labor inside myself, and I have become to myself a piece of difficult ground, not to be worked over without much sweat. For we are not now examining the regions of the heaven or measuring the distances of the stars or inquiring into how the earth is balanced in space. It is I myself who remember, I, the mind. There is nothing remarkable in the fact that something other than myself is far away from me; but what can be nearer to me than my own self? Yet this force of my memory is incomprehensible to me, even though, without it, I should not be able to call myself myself. What am I to say, when I see so clearly that I remember forgetfulness? Shall I say that what I remember is not in my memory? Or that forgetfulness is in my memory in order that I should not forget? Both answers are absurd. Is the third possibility any better? Could I say that it is the image of forgetfulness, not forgetfulness itself, which is held by my memory when I remember it? No, I could not; since when the image of a thing is impressed on the memory, it is first of all necessary that the thing itself should be present from which the impression can be derived. In this way I remember Carthage, or any other place where I have been; in this way I remember the faces of people I have seen and all things reported to me by the other senses; so too I remember the health or sickness of the body. When these things were present, the memory received their images from them and these images remained present for me to contemplate and bring back to mind when I recollected the objects themselves, which were absent. If, therefore, forgetfulness is retained in the memory by means of an image, and not in itself, then undoubtedly forgetfulness must at some time have been present so that its image could be received. But how, when it was present, could it inscribe its image on the memory, when its presence means the destruction even of all records that are already there? Nevertheless, however it may be, however incomprehensible and inexplicable, I am quite sure that I do remember this forgetfulness by which what we remember is effaced.

17

GREAT INDEED is the power of memory! It is something terrifying, my God, a profound and infinite multiplicity; and this thing is the mind, and this thing is I myself. What then am I, my God? What is my nature? A life various, manifold, and quite immeasurable. Imagine the plains, caverns, and abysses of my memory; they are innumerable and are innumerably full of innumerable kinds of things, present either in their images, as in the case of all bodies, or in themselves, as with the arts, or in the form of some kind of notion or consciousness, as with the affections of the mind, which, even when the mind is not experiencing them, are still retained by the memory (though whatever is in the memory is also in the mind). Through all this I range; I fly here and I fly there; I dive down deep as I can, and I can find no end. So great is the force of memory, so great is the force of life in man who lives to die.

What shall I do, you true life of mine, my God? I will go past this force of mine called memory; I will go beyond it so that I may draw nearer to you, sweet light. What is it that you are saying to me? I mount up through my mind toward you who dwell above me, and now I shall go beyond this force of mine called memory, for I desire to reach you at the point from which you may be reached, to cling to you at the point from which it is possible for me to cling to you. For even beasts and birds have memory; otherwise they would not be able to find their ways back to their dens and nests or do any of the other things they are used to doing; indeed without memory they could not become used to doing anything. So I will pass beyond memory also, so that I may reach him who separated me from the four-footed beasts and made me wiser than the birds of the air. I will pass beyond memory to find you—Oh where, where, shall I find you, my truly good, my certain loveliness? If I find you beyond my memory, I can have no memory of you. And how shall I find you if I do not remember you?

18

THE WOMAN who had lost her groat sought for it with a light; but unless she had remembered it, she would not have found it. For when it was discovered, how could she have known whether it was the right one or not, if she had not remembered it? I remember many occasions when I have looked for and found something which I had lost, and from these experiences I know that when I was looking for the thing and people asked me: "Is this it?" or "Is that it?" I would go on saying: "No, it is not," until the thing that I really was looking for was produced. But unless I had remembered it, whatever it was, I would not have found it even if it were produced in front of me, since I would not have recognized it. And this is always the case when we look for and find something that was lost. If something happens to disappear from the eyes and not from the memory (as any visible body), its image is retained within us and is looked for until it is restored to sight, and when found, it is recognized by the image that is within. We do not say that we have found what was lost unless we recognize it, and we cannot recognize it unless we remember it. It was certainly lost to the eyes, but it was still held in the memory.

19

BUT WHEN THE MEMORY itself loses something, as happens when we forget a thing and try to recollect it, where can we possibly look for it except in the memory? And there if something other than what we are looking for is presented to us, we reject it until the thing that we are looking for turns up. And when it does turn up we say: "This is it." We would not say this unless we recognized it, and we would not recognize it unless we remembered it. Yet certainly we had forgotten it.

Or could this be the solution: the whole thing had not slipped from our memory; part of it was retained and by means of this part the other part was sought for, because the memory realized that it was not carrying along with it the totality which it was used to and, going unevenly, as it were, through the loss of something to which it was accustomed, eagerly demanded the restoration of what was lacking. For instance if we see or think of some man who is known to us, but have forgotten his name and are trying to recall it, any name that occurs to us other than his will not fit in, because we are not in the habit of thinking of that name and that person together. Consequently we go on rejecting names until the name presents itself with which our knowledge can rest satisfied, since it is the name with which it was accustomed to make the appropriate connection. And that name cannot come from any other source except the memory. Even when we recognize it after being reminded of it by someone else, the recognition still comes from the memory. We do not accept it as though it were something new; instead we agree that this was what it was because we remember it to be so. If it were entirely blotted out of our mind, we should not remember it even when reminded of it. For if we can remember that we have forgotten something, this means that we have not entirely forgotten it. Whatever has been utterly forgotten cannot even be thought of as lost and cannot be sought for.

20

How, THEN, LORD, do I seek you? For when I seek you, my God, I am seeking the happy life. *I will seek Thee, that my soul may live.* For my body lives by my soul, and my soul lives by you. How, then, do I seek for the happy life? For I cannot find it until I can reach the place where I can truly say: "It is enough; it is there." How then, do I seek it? Is it by remembrance, as though I had forgotten it but can still remember that I have forgotten? Or is it through desire to learn something unknown, something which either I never knew or which I have so completely forgotten that I cannot even remember that I have forgotten it? Is not the happy life the thing that all men desire, literally every single man without exception? But where did they get the knowledge of it, that they should desire it so? Where did they see it, that they should love it so? We have it, certainly; but how we have it, I do not know. In one sense a person may reach a certain degree of happiness and be called happy; others are happy in the hope of happiness. These latter

162   *The Confessions of St. Augustine*

do not have it in the same full sense as those who actually possess it; but they are better off than those who are neither happy in fact nor in hope. Though even these last must have it in some sense or other; otherwise they would not (as they certainly do) have such a wish to be happy. In some way or other they know of it and, therefore, may be said to possess it in some form of knowledge. Is this form of knowledge, I inquire, in the memory? If it is, then we must have experienced happiness at some time previously. I am not now asking whether this is an experience which we have all had individually, or whether the experience was in that man who first sinned, in whom we all died and of whom we are all born in misery. I am only asking whether the happy life is in our memory. For we could not love it, if we did not know it. We have heard the name "happiness" and all of us would agree that we desire the thing signified by the name; for it is not simply the sound of the word that pleases us. If a Greek hears the word in Latin, he derives no pleasure from it, since he does not know what has been said; but we are pleased, just in the same way as he would have been if he had heard the word in Greek. For the thing itself is neither Greek nor Latin, but it is something which Greeks, Latins, and men of all other languages long to attain. It is therefore known to all of them, and if they could all be asked with one voice: "Do you wish to be happy?" they would without any doubt reply, "We do." And this would not be so unless the thing itself, signified by the word, was contained in their memory.

21

BUT IS THIS an example of the same kind of memory as when I, who have seen Carthage, remember Carthage? No, it is not; for the happy life, not being a body, is not visible to our eyes. Do we then remember it in the same way as we remember numbers? No, we do not; whoever has a knowledge of numbers is content with that and need seek no further; but we who have a knowledge of the happy life and therefore love it, do want to go further so that we may reach it and become happy. Is it, then, as we remember eloquence? No, it is not. Though it is true that on hearing the word "eloquence" many people, who have not yet become eloquent, call to mind the thing signified by the word and many people would like to be eloquent—all of which shows that the thing is in their knowledge; yet it is by means of the bodily senses that they have observed others who are eloquent, have been pleased by it, and have wanted to become eloquent themselves (though unless they had some interior notion, they would not be pleased, and, if they were not pleased, they would not want to possess this quality); however, there is no bodily sense which enables us to experience the happy life in others. Do we, then, remember it as we remember joy? This is possible. For I remember my joy even when I am sad, just as I remember the happy life even when I am unhappy. And never by any bodily sense did I see my joy, or hear it or smell it or taste it or touch it. I experienced it in my mind at the time when I was joyful, and the knowledge of it stuck in my memory so that I can call it back to mind, sometimes with contempt, sometimes with longing, according to the diversity of the things which I remember enjoying. For even base and disgraceful things have filled me with a kind of joy—things which now I detest and execrate when I recall them— and at other times I have had joy in good and worthy things which I remember with longing, though they may not be with me any more, so that I am sad when I recall the joy of the past.

Where, then, was it, and when was it that I experienced my happy life, so that I should remember it and love it and long for it? And not I alone, or I and a few others, but all of us; we all want to be happy. And unless we knew it with certain knowledge, we could not wish for it with so certain a will. But here is another point. Suppose two men are asked whether they want to join the army: it might happen that one would say "Yes" and the other would say "No." But if they are asked whether they want to be happy, both, without any doubt, would immediately say "Yes," and the only reason why one of them wanted to join the army and the other did not, was that they both wanted to be happy. Is it perhaps the case that different things make different people joyful and that so all agree that they want to be happy, just as they would agree, if they were asked, that they wanted to feel joy? And they think that joy itself is the same thing as the happy life? One may attain joy in one way, another in another way, but the end at which they are all aiming is one and the same, namely, a state of joy. And joy is something which no one can say he has no experience of; therefore, he finds it in his memory and recognizes it when he hears the words: "the happy life."

22

FAR BE IT, LORD, far be it from the heart of your servant who is confessing to you, far be it that I should think that any joy that I may experience makes me happy! For there is a joy that is not given to the ungodly, but only to those who love you for your own sake,

and you yourself are their joy. And this is the happy life—
to rejoice in you and to you and because of you. This is
the happy life; there is no other. And those who think
there is another, are in pursuit of another joy which is not
the true joy. Yet all the same their will is still involved
with some kind of an image of joy.

23

So IT IS NOT certain that all men want to be happy.
Those who do not want to find their joy in you (which
alone is the happy life) certainly do not want the happy
life. Or do all men really desire it, but *because the
flesh lusteth against the Spirit and the Spirit against the
flesh, that they cannot do what they would,* they fall into
that state which is within their powers and are content
with it because their will for a state which is beyond
them is not strong enough to bring it within their reach?
For if I ask anyone: "Would you rather have your joy in
truth or in falsehood?" he would say: "In truth," with
just as little hesitation as he would say that he wants to be
happy. And certainly the happy life is joy in truth, which
means joy in you, who are truth, God, *my light, health of
my countenance, my God.* This is the happy life which all
desire; this life which alone is happy all desire; joy in
truth is what all desire. I have met many people who
wanted to deceive, but no one who wanted to be deceived.
But where did they gain their knowledge of this happy
life except in the place where they also gained their
knowledge of truth? For they love truth also (because
they do not want to be deceived) and in loving the
happy life (which simply means joy in truth) they must
certainly love truth too, and they would not be able to

love it, unless there were some knowledge of it in their memory. Why, then, do they not find their joy in it? Why are they not happy? Because they are more strongly taken up by other things which have more power to make them unhappy than that, which they so dimly remember, has to make them happy. For there is still only a little light in men, and they must walk, yes, they must *walk, that the darkness overtake them not.*

But why is it that "truth gives birth to hatred"? Why does your servant who preaches the truth incur enmity in spite of the fact that people love the happy life which simply is joy in truth? It is because truth is loved in such a way that those who love something else would like to believe that what they love is the truth, and because they would not like to be deceived, they object to being shown that in fact they are deceived. And so they hate truth for the sake of whatever it is they love instead of truth. They love the light of truth, but hate it when it shows them up as wrong. Because they do not want to be deceived and do want to deceive, they love truth when truth is giving evidence, but hate it when the evidence given is against themselves. And the retribution which will come to them is this: those who do not want to stand in the light of truth, will have to stand in it, whether they like it or not, but truth will not reveal her light to them. So it is, yes, so indeed it is: this human mind of ours, so blind and sick, so foul and ill-favored, wants to be hidden itself, but hates to have anything hidden from it. But what happens is just the contrary: it cannot hide from truth, but truth can be out of its sight. Yet even so, wretched as it is, it prefers to find joy in truth than in falsehoods. It will be happy, therefore, when, with no

distractions to interpose themselves, it will find its joy in
that only truth by which all things are true.

24

SEE WHAT A DISTANCE I have covered searching for
you, Lord, in my memory! And I have not found you
outside it. Nor have I found anything about you which
I have not kept in my memory from the time I first
learned you. For from the time I learned you, I have not
forgotten you. For when I found truth, then I found my
God, truth itself, and from the time I learned it I have
not forgotten it. And so, since the time I learned you,
you stay in my memory, and there I find you whenever I call you to mind and delight in you. There are my
holy delights, which in your mercy you have given me,
having regard to my poverty.

25

BUT WHERE IS IT, LORD, in my memory that you stay?
In what part of it do you stay? What resting place have
you framed for yourself? What sanctuary have you built?
You have given my memory the honor of staying in it:
but in what part of it do you stay? This is what I now
consider.

While I was calling you to mind, I went beyond those
parts of the memory which the beasts also have (because
I did not find you there among the images of material
things), and I came to those parts of it where I had stored
up the affections of my mind, but did not find you there
either. And I went into the seat of the mind itself (which
the mind has in my memory, since the mind remembers
itself), and you were not there. For, just as you are not a

material image, nor an affection of any living man (such as we feel when we are in a state of joy, sorrow, desire, fear, memory, forgetfulness, or anything else of this kind), so you are not the mind itself, because you are the Lord God of the mind, and all these things change, but you remain changeless over all things, and you have deigned to dwell in my memory, from the time I first learned of you. And why do I inquire in what place of my memory you dwell, as though there were any places there? Certainly you do dwell in my memory, because I remember you from the time I first learned of you, and I find you there when I call you to mind.

26

WHERE THEN did I find you, so that I could learn of you? For you were not in my memory before I learned of you. Where then did I find you, so that I could learn of you? I could only have found you in yourself, above me. Place there is none; we go *backward and forward,* and there is no place. Truth, you are everywhere in session, ready to listen to all who ask counsel of you, and at one and the same moment you give your answer to every diversity of question. You answer clearly, though everyone does not hear clearly. All ask what they wish, but they do not always hear what they want to hear. He serves you best who is not so anxious to hear from you what he wills as to will what he hears from you.

27

LATE IT WAS that I loved you, beauty so ancient and so new, late I loved you! And, look, you were within me and I was outside, and there I sought for you and in my ugliness I plunged into the beauties that you have made. You were with me, and I was not with you. Those outer beauties kept me far from you, yet if they had not been in you, they would not have existed at all. You called, you cried out, you shattered my deafness: you flashed, you shone, you scattered my blindness: you breathed perfume, and I drew in my breath and I pant for you: I tasted, and I am hungry and thirsty: you touched me, and I burned for your peace.

28

WHEN IN MY whole self I shall cling to you united, I shall find no sorrow anywhere, no labor; wholly alive will my life be all full of you. Those whom you fill, you raise up, and now, since I am not yet full of you, I am a burden to myself. Joys in which I should find sorrow conflict with sorrows in which I should find joy, and on which side stands the victory I do not know. I am sad for myself. Lord, have pity on me! My evil sorrows conflict with my good joys, and on which side stands the victory I do not know. I am sad for myself. Lord, have pity on me! I am sad for myself. Look, I am not hiding my wounds: you are the doctor and I am sick; you are merciful, I need mercy. *Is not the life of man upon earth all trial?* Does anyone want to be in trouble and difficulties? These you order us to endure, not to love. No one loves what he endures, even though he loves to endure. For however much he may rejoice in the fact of his endurance, he would still prefer that there were nothing to endure. In adversity I long for prosperity, in prosperity I fear adversity. What middle place is there between these two when the life of man is not all trial? All the prosperities of this world are cursed once and again—by the fear of adversity and by the corruption of joy. And the adversities of this world are cursed once, twice, and three times—by the longing for prosperity, by the very bitterness of adversity itself, and by the fear that it may break down our endurance. Is it not true, then, that the life of man upon earth is all trial without intermission?

29

AND ALL MY HOPE is nowhere except in your great mercy. Grant us what you command, and command us what you will. You demand that we should be continent. And *when I knew,* as it is said, *that no man can be continent, unless God give it, this also was a part of wisdom to know whose gift she is.* Certainly it is by continence that we are brought together and brought back to the One, after having dissipated ourselves among the Many. For he loves you insufficiently who loves something else with you which he does not love for your sake. O love, ever burning, and never extinguished, charity, my God, set me on fire! You command continence. Grant what you command, and command what you will.

30

CERTAINLY you command me to restrain myself from the *lust of the flesh, the lust of the eyes, and the ambition of the world.* You commanded me to abstain from sleeping with a mistress, and with regard to marriage you advised me to take a better course than the one that was permitted me. And since you gave me the power, it was done, even before I became a dispenser of your Sacrament. But there still live in that memory of mine, of which I have spoken so much, images of the things which my habit has fixed there. These images come into my thoughts, and, though when I am awake they are strengthless, in sleep they not only cause pleasure but go so far as to obtain assent and something very like reality. These images, though real, have such an effect on my soul, in my flesh, that false visions in my sleep obtain from me what true visions cannot when I am awake. Surely, Lord my God, I am myself when I am asleep? And yet there is a very great difference between myself and myself in that moment of time when I pass from being awake to being asleep or come back again from sleep to wakefulness. Where then is my reason which, when I am awake, resists such suggestions and remains unshaken if the realities themselves were presented to it? Do reason's eyes close with the eyes of the body? Does reason go to sleep when the bodily senses sleep? If so, how does it happen that even in our sleep we do often resist and, remembering our purpose and most chastely abiding by it, give no assent to enticements of this kind? Nevertheless, there is a great difference, because, when it happens otherwise, we return on waking to a peace of conscience and, by the very remoteness of our state now and then, discover that it was not we who did something which was, to our regret, somehow or other done in us.

Almighty God, surely your hand is powerful enough to cure all the sicknesses of my soul and, with a more abundant measure of your grace, to quench even the lustful impulses of my sleep. Lord, you will increase your gifts in me more and more, so that my soul, disentangled from the birdlime of concupiscence, may follow me to you; so that it may not be in revolt against itself and may not, even in dreams, succumb to or even give the slightest assent to those degrading corruptions which by means of sensual images actually disturb and pollute the flesh. It is not a hard thing for you, Almighty, who are *able to do above all that we ask or think,* to prevent anything of this sort, not even the very slightest inclination (so small that a mere nod would check it), from affecting the chaste mind of a sleeper—and to prevent it not only in this life but at this age at which I am now. But now I have explained to my good Lord what is still my state in this kind of evil, *rejoicing with trembling* in your gifts and grieving for my imperfection and hoping that you will perfect your mercies in me till I reach that fullness of peace which both my inward and my outer self will have with you when *death shall be swallowed up in victory.*

31

THERE IS ANOTHER *evil of the day,* and I wish that it were *sufficient for it.* It is by eating and drinking that we repair the losses suffered by the body every day until the time comes when you *destroy both belly and meat,* when you kill all need with a wonderful fullness, and *clothe this corruptible* with an eternal *incorruption.* But now this necessity is sweet to me, and I fight against this sweetness, so that I may not become its prisoner; by fasting I carry on war every day, often *bringing my body into subjection,* and the pain I suffer in this way is driven out by pleasure. For hunger and thirst are pains; they burn us up and kill us like a fever, unless we are relieved by the medicine of nourishment. And this nourishment is at hand by the consolation of your gifts, in which earth and water and sky serve our weakness, and so our calamity is called our delight.

This you have taught me, that I should have the same attitude toward taking food as I have toward taking medicine. But while I pass from the discomfort of hunger to the satisfaction of sufficiency, in that very moment of transition there is set for me a snare of concupiscence. For the moment of transition is pleasurable, and we are forced to go through that moment; there is no other way. And while we eat and drink for the sake of health, there is a dangerous kind of pleasure which follows in attendance on health and very often tries to put itself first, so that what I say that I am doing, and mean to do, for the sake of my health is actually done for the sake of pleasure. Nor is there the same measure for both; what is enough for health is not enough for pleasure, and it is often hard to tell whether it is the necessary care of my body asking for sustenance or whether it is a deceitful voluptuousness of greed trying to seduce me. And because of this uncertainty the unhappy soul is delighted; it uses it as a cover and excuse for itself, and is glad that it is not clearly evident what is sufficient for a healthy moderation, so that under the cloak of health it may hide the business of pleasure. Every day I try to resist these temptations; I call upon your right hand to help me, and I refer my perplexities to you, since I have not yet found a settled plan in this matter.

I hear the voice of my God commanding: *Let not your hearts be overcharged with surfeiting and drunkenness.* I have no inclination to drunkenness, and in your mercy you will keep me far from it; but overeating has sometimes crept up on your servant. You will have mercy, so that it may be far from me. For *no one can be continent unless you give it.* You give us many things that we pray for, and everything good that we receive before we pray we receive at your hands. I have never been a drunkard, but I have known drunkards who have been made sober by you. Therefore, it is your doing that some men have never been drunkards; it is your doing that others who have been drunkards should not always remain so, and it is also your doing that both sorts of men should know that it is your doing.

I heard another voice of yours: *Go not after thy lusts, and from thy pleasure turn away.* This too, by your gift, I heard and I have greatly loved it: *Neither if we eat, shall we abound; neither if we eat not, shall we lack,* that is to say, the one will not make me rich and the other will not make me miserable. And I heard too: *For I have learned in whatever state I am, therewith to be content; I know how to abound, and how to suffer need. I can do all things through Christ that strengtheneth me.* There indeed speaks one who is a soldier of the heavenly army, not dust, as we are. But *remember,* Lord, *that we are dust,* and that *of dust Thou hast made man,* and *he was lost and is found.* Nor did he do it by his own power (since he was the same dust)—he, I mean, whom I loved so much when he said such things through the breath of your inspiration. *I can do all things,* he says, *through Him that strengtheneth me.* Strengthen me, so that I can. Give what you command, and command what you will. Paul confesses that he has received, and when he glories, it is in the Lord that he glories. I have heard another also begging that he might receive: *Take from me,* he says, *the desires of the belly.* From which, O holy God, it appears that it is your gift when what you command to be done is done.

Good Father, you have taught me that *to the pure all things are pure;* but that *it is evil unto the man that eateth with offense,* and, that *every creature of Thine is good, and nothing to be refused, which is received with thanks-*

giving, and that *meat commendeth us not to God,* and, that *no man should judge as in meat or drink,* and that *he which eateth, let him not despise him that eateth not, and let not him that eateth not, judge him that eateth.* These things I have learned, thanks and praise to you, my God, my master, knocking at my ears, enlightening my heart; deliver me from all temptation. It is not any uncleanness in the meat that I fear; it is the uncleanness of gluttony. I know that Noah was allowed to eat all kinds of meat that are good for food; that Elijah was fed with meat; that John the Baptist, who was endowed with the most remarkable abstinence, was not polluted by the living creatures, locusts, which were given him for food. I know too that Esau was deceived because of his greediness for lentils; that David reproached himself for desiring some water, and that our King was tempted not with meat, but with bread. And the reason why the Israelites in the wilderness deserved to be blamed was not because they desired meat but because, in desiring food, they murmured against the Lord.

Placed as I am among these temptations, I strive every day against concupiscence in eating and drinking; for this is not the sort of thing that I can decide to give up once and for all and never touch again, as I was able to do with sex. Therefore, I must keep a hold which is neither too loose nor too tight on the bridle of my throat. And it is scarcely possible, Lord, not to be carried slightly beyond the bounds of necessity. Anyone who can keep exactly within them is a great man and greatly should he praise your name. But I am not he, since I am a sinful man. Yet I too magnify your name, and *He maketh intercession to Thee* for my sins who *hath overcome the world;* numbering me among the *weak members* of His *body;* because

Thine eyes have seen that of Him which is *imperfect, and in Thy book shall all be written.*

32

AS TO THE ENTICEMENTS which come to us from the sense of smell, I am not much concerned with them. I do not miss them when they are absent, or reject them when they are present, and I am quite prepared to be without them altogether. So it seems to me, though I may be deceiving myself. For here too there is a sad kind of darkness, the darkness in which the abilities that are in me are hidden from me, so that when my mind questions itself about its own powers, it cannot be certain that its replies are trustworthy, because what is inside the mind is mostly hidden and remains hidden until revealed by experience, and in this life, which is described as a continuous trial, no one ought to feel sure that, just as he has been worse and become better, he may not also, after having been better, become worse. Our one hope, our one confidence, our one firm promise is your mercy.

33

THE DELIGHTS of the sense of hearing had a stronger grip and a greater authority over me; but you loosed the bond and set me free. Yet now when I hear sung in a sweet and well-trained voice those melodies into which your words breathe life, I do, I admit, feel some pleasurable relaxation, though not of the kind which would make it difficult for me to tear myself away, for I could get up and leave when I like. Nevertheless they do demand a place of some dignity in my heart so that they may be received into me together with the words that give them life, and it is not easy for me to give them exactly the right place. For sometimes it seems to me that I am giving them more honor than is right. I may feel that when these holy words themselves are well sung, our minds are stirred up more fervently and more religiously into a flame of devotion than if they are not so well sung, and I realize that the emotions of the spirit are various, each, by some secret kind of correspondence, capable of being excited by its own proper mode of voice or song. But I am often deceived by this pleasure of my flesh, to which the mind should not be given over to be enervated. The bodily sense only deserves to be admitted because of the reason; but often, instead of being content to follow behind reason, it tries to go ahead of reason and take the lead. So in these matters I sin without realizing it, only realizing afterward that I have sinned.

But at other times, when I am overanxious to avoid being deceived in this way, I fall into the error of being too severe—so much so that I would like banished both from my own ears and those of the Church as well the whole melody of sweet music that is used with David's Psalter—and the safer course seems to me that of Athanasius, bishop of Alexandria, who, as I have often been told, made the reader of the psalm employ so very small a modulation of the voice that the effect was more like speaking than singing. But then I remember the tears I shed at the singing in church at the time when I was beginning to recover my faith; I remember that now I am moved not by the singing but by the things that are sung, when they are sung with a clear voice and correct modulation, and once again I recognize the great utility of this institution. So I fluctuate between the danger of pleasure and my experience of the good that can be done. I am inclined on the whole (though I do not regard this opinion as irrevocable) to be in favor of the practice of singing in church, so that by means of the delight in hearing the weaker minds may be roused to a feeling of devotion. Nevertheless, whenever it happens to me that I am more moved by the singing than by what is sung, I confess that I am sinning grievously, and then I would prefer not to hear the music. See what a state I am in! I hope that you will weep with me and weep for me, all those of you who have inside you some of the good feeling from which good actions come. Those of you who have not, will not be moved by these things. And I pray that you, my Lord God, will hear me and look down upon me and see me and cure me. In your eyes I have become a problem to myself, and *that is my infirmity.*

34

THERE REMAINS the pleasure of these eyes of my flesh, and it is of this pleasure that I now make my confessions in the hearing of the ears of your temple— those brotherly and devout ears. With this I shall conclude the account of the temptations arising from *the lust of the flesh,* temptations which still beset me, *groaning earnestly, and desiring to be clothed with my house that is from heaven.*

The eyes love beautiful shapes of all kinds, glowing and delightful colors. These things must not take hold on my soul; that is for God to do. Certainly God made these things very good, but it is He Himself, not these things, who is my good. These things affect me during all the time every day that I am awake. I get no respite from them, as I get from the sounds of music and sometimes, in silence, from all sounds. For light is the queen of colors, and wherever I am in daytime she is suffused over everything visible; she glides up to me in shape after shape, cajoling me when I am doing something quite different and am paying no deliberate attention to her. But she makes her way so forcibly into my mind that, if light is suddenly withdrawn, I look for it again with longing, and if it is absent for long, my mind grows sad.

Let me think of that light which Tobias saw when, with these eyes shut, he showed his son the way of life and, with the feet of charity, went in front of him and never missed the path. Or the light which Isaac saw when, with his fleshly eyes heavy and dim with age, it was granted him to bless his sons without being able to see which was which, and yet in the act of blessing to gain the power of distinguishing between them. Or the light which Jacob saw when he also had become blind through great age; yet his heart was illumined and in the persons of his sons he shed light on the tribes of the future which were foreshadowed by them, and he laid his hands, mystically reversed, on his grandchildren, the sons of Joseph, not as their father, seeing from without, directed, but according to his own inner discernment. This is light itself; it is one, and all who see it and love it are one. As to that corporeal light, of which I was speaking, it is a tempting and dangerous sweetness, like a sauce spread over the life of this world for its blind lovers. Yet those who know how to praise you for this light, "Creator Thou of everything," carry it up to you in your hymn, and are not carried away by it into spiritual sleep. So I would like to be. I resist these seductions of the eyes, so that my feet with which I walk your way may not be ensnared, and to you I lift up my invisible eyes, so that you may *pluck my feet out of the snare.* Repeatedly you do pluck them out, for they are ensnared. You do not cease to pluck them out, while I so frequently entangle myself in the traps spread around me on all sides; because *Thou that keepest Israel shalt neither slumber nor sleep.*

And to the temptations of the eyes, men themselves in their various arts and manufactures have made innumerable additions: clothes, shoes, vases, products of craftsmanship; pictures too and all sorts of statues—far beyond what is necessary for use, moderate or with any religious meaning. So men go outside themselves to follow things of their own making, and inside themselves they are forsaking Him who made them and are destroying what they themselves were made to be. But I, my God and my glory, find here also something from which to make a hymn to you, and I offer my praise in sacrifice to Him who sanctifies me. Because all those beauties which pass through men's souls into their skillful hands come from that Beauty which is above souls and for which my soul is sighing day and night. From it artists and enthusiasts for external beauties derive the criterion by which to judge what is beautiful or not, but they do not find the rule for making the right use of these forms of beauty. Yet the rule is there, though they do not see it—a rule telling them not to go too far, and to keep their strength for you instead of dissipating it upon delights that end in lassitude. Yet I who am saying this and who see the truth of what I say still entangle my steps in these outer beauties. But you will pluck me out, Lord, you will pluck me out, *because Thy loving kindness is before my eyes.* For I am most pitifully caught up by them, but you will pity me and pluck me out, and sometimes, when I am only lightly caught in the trap, I scarcely realize what you are doing; sometimes, when I have become deeply implicated, I feel pain.

35

I MUST NOW mention another form of temptation which is in many ways more dangerous. Apart from the concupiscence of the flesh which is present in the delight we take in all the pleasures of the senses (and the slaves of it perish as they put themselves far from you), there is also present in the soul, by means of these same bodily senses, a kind of empty longing and curiosity which aims not at taking pleasure in the flesh but at acquiring experience through the flesh, and this empty curiosity is dignified by the names of learning and science. Since this is in the appetite for knowing, and since the eyes are the chief of our senses for acquiring knowledge, it is called in the divine language *the lust of the eyes*. For "to see" is used properly of the eyes; but we also use this word of the other senses when we are employing them for the purpose of gaining knowledge. We do not say: "Hear how it flashes" or "Smell how bright it is" or "Taste how it shines" or "Feel how it gleams"; in all these cases we use the verb "to see." But we not only say: "See how it shines," a thing which can only be perceived by the eyes; we also say "See how it sounds," "See how it smells," "See how it tastes," "See how hard it is." Therefore, the general experience of the senses is, as was said before, called "the lust of the eyes," because seeing, which belongs properly to the eyes, is used by analogy of the other senses too when they are attempting to discover any kind of knowledge.

In this it is easy to see how pleasure and curiosity have different objects in their use of the senses. Pleasure goes after what is beautiful to us, sweet to hear, to smell, to taste, to touch; but curiosity, for the sake of experiment, may go after the exact opposites of these, not in order to suffer discomfort, but simply because of the lust to find out and to know. What pleasure can there be in looking at a mangled corpse, which must excite our horror? Yet if there is one near, people flock to see it, so as to grow sad and pale at the sight. They are actually frightened of seeing it in their sleep, as though anyone had forced them to see it when they were awake or as if they had been induced to look at it because it had the reputation of being a beautiful thing to see. The same is true of the other senses. There is no need to go to the length of producing examples. Because of this disease of curiosity monsters and anything out of the ordinary are put on show in our theaters. From the same motive men proceed to investigate the workings of nature which is beyond our ken—things which it does no good to know and which men only want to know for the sake of knowing. So too, and with this same end of perverted science, people make inquiries by means of magic. Even in religion we find the same thing: God is tempted when signs and portents are demanded and are not desired for any salutory purpose, but simply for the experience of seeing them.

In this enormous forest, so full of snares and dangers, many are the temptations which I have cut off and thrust away from my heart, as you, God of my salvation, have granted me the power. Yet since so many things of this kind are buzzing around our daily life in all directions, how can I dare to say, how can I ever dare to say that nothing of this sort can make me give my attention to it or fill me with the empty desire to possess it? True that I am no longer carried away by the theater; I am not interested in knowing about the courses of the stars; my soul has never made inquiries from the ghosts of the dead; I detest all sacrilegious mysteries. Yet, my Lord God, to whom I owe my humble and pure service, there are all kinds of artifices of suggestion by which the enemy urges me to seek for some sign from you. But I beg you by our King and by our country Jerusalem, the chaste and pure, that just as up to now it has been far from me to give my assent to such suggestions, so the possibility of doing so may become more and more remote. But when I pray to you for the good of someone else my mind is directed to a quite different end; you do as you will, and you give and will give me the grace cheerfully to accept your will.

Nevertheless, there are very many occasions, small and contemptible enough, in which this curiosity of ours is tempted every day, and it is impossible to count the times when we slip. It often happens that people talk to us in some empty idle way, and we listen to them tolerantly at first, so as not to give offense to the weak; but then we gradually begin to take a serious interest in their gossip. I no longer go to the Games to see a dog coursing a hare; but if I happen to be going through the country and see this sport going on, it may attract my attention away from some serious meditation—not so much as to make me turn my horse's body out of the way, but enough to alter the inclination of my mind. And unless you showed me my infirmity and quickly admonished me either by some thought connected with the sight itself to rise up toward you, or else to pay no attention to the thing at all and to pass by, I should stand there empty-headed like a stock. And then there are all the occasions when I am sitting at home and my attention is attracted by a lizard catching flies or by a spider entangling them in his web.

The animals may be small, but this does not make the thing any different. I go on from them to praise you, wonderful Creator and Director of all things; but it was not this that first drew my attention. It is one thing to get up quickly and another thing not to fall down. My life is full of such things and my only hope is in your great, great mercy. For when our heart is made the receptacle for things of this kind and becomes laden with pressing throngs of vanity, the result is that even our prayers are interrupted and disturbed, and when, in your presence, we are directing the voice of our heart to your ears, our great and serious purpose is broken off by an invasion of idle empty thoughts, coming from I know not where.

36

CERTAINLY WE CANNOT regard this as among things of little importance. And there is nothing to bring us back to hope except your known mercy, since you have begun to change us.

And you know how far you have already changed me, you who first cured me of my lust for asserting myself against others, so that you may be merciful also to the rest of my iniquities, *and heal all my infirmities, and redeem my life from corruption, and crown me with mercy and pity, and satisfy my desire with good things:* you who curbed my pride with your fear and tamed my neck to your yoke. And now I bear that yoke and I find it light. This was what you promised and this is what you have done. And indeed it always was light, though I did not know it in the time when I was afraid to take it upon me.

But tell me, Lord, you who alone are Lord without

pride, because you are alone the true Lord, who has no other Lord, has this third kind of temptation disappeared from me, or can it ever entirely disappear in this life? I mean the wish to be feared and loved by men for no other reason but to get from it a joy, which is no true joy. It is a wretched way of life, a disgusting kind of ostentation. Here in particular we may find the reason why you are not purely loved or feared, and therefore *dost Thou resist the proud, and givest grace to the humble,* and you thunder down upon the ambitions of this world, and *the foundations of the mountains tremble.* And so, because there are certain positions in human society where the holder of office must be loved and feared by men, the enemy of our true happiness is always close upon us, setting his snares everywhere in the words "Well done, well done," and hoping that, while we greedily snatch at them, we shall be taken unawares, shall no longer plan our joy in your truth but shall entrust it to the deceitfulness of men, and shall want to be loved and feared not because of you but instead of you. In this way our enemy will make us become like him and will have us united to him not in the bonds of charity but in the bonds of punishment—he who decided to *set his throne in the north,* so that there, in cold and darkness, men might become his slaves as he attempts pervertedly and crookedly to imitate you. But as to us, Lord, see, we are your *little flock.* Keep us in your possession. Stretch out your wings so that we may take refuge beneath them. It is you who must be our glory; let us be loved for your sake, and let it be your word that is feared in us. The man who wishes to be praised by men regardless of your approval will not be defended by men when you judge him, nor delivered by men when you condemn him. It may not be the case of a *sinner being praised in the desires of his soul* or a man *blessed who doth ungodlily;* it may be that a man is praised for some gift which you have given him and takes more pleasure in hearing himself praised than in having that gift for which he is praised; this man too is praised by men, but blamed by you, and those who praise him are better than he who is praised; for what gives them pleasure is the gift of God in a man, but he takes more pleasure in what men give than in what God has given.

37

WE ARE TEMPTED, LORD, by these temptations every day; without intermission we are tempted. The tongue of man is the furnace in which we are tried every day. Here too you command us to be continent. Give what you command, and command what you will. You know how on this matter my heart groans to you and my eyes stream tears. For I cannot easily discover how far I have become cleaner from this disease, and I much fear my hidden sins which are visible to your eyes, though not to mine. For in other kinds of temptation I have at least some means of finding out about myself; but in this kind it is almost impossible. With regard to the pleasures of the flesh and the unnecessary curiosity for knowledge I can see how far I have advanced in the ability to control my mind simply by observing myself when I am without these things, either from choice or when they are not available. For I can then ask myself how much or how little I mind not having them. So too with regard to riches, which are desired for the satisfaction of one or two or all of those three concupiscences; if one is not able to be quite sure in one's own mind whether or not one despises them when one has them, it is possible to get rid of them so as to put oneself to the test. But how can we arrange things so as to be without praise and make the same experiment with regard to it? Are we to live a bad life, to live in such a wicked and abandoned way that everyone who knows us will detest us? Nothing could be madder than such a suggestion as that. On the contrary, if praise both goes with and ought to go with a good life and good works, we should no more part with it than with the good life itself. Yet unless a thing is not there I cannot tell whether it is difficult or easy for me to be without it.

With regard to this kind of temptation then, what, Lord, shall I confess? This I can say, that I take pleasure in praise, but more pleasure in truth than in praise. For if I were given the choice of either being out of my wits and wrong on every subject, yet praised by everyone, or being firm and sure in the truth, yet abused by everyone, I know which I should choose. Yet I wish it were not the case that when someone else praises me, my joy in whatever good quality I may have is increased. It is increased however, I admit; not only that, but it is diminished by dispraise. And when I am troubled at this wretched state of mine, an excuse occurs to me, whether it is a good one or not, you, God, know; for it leaves me uncertain. You demand from us not only continence— that is, to restrain our love from certain things—but also justice—that is, to direct our love upon certain things— and it is your will not only that we should love you but also that we should love our neighbor. So it often seems to me that when I am pleased by intelligent praise I am pleased because of the sound judgment or the promise shown by my neighbor, and in the same way it is his faults that make me sad when I hear him dispraise something which he does not understand or which is good. For there are also times when I feel sad to hear myself praised, either when people praise things in me which I dislike in myself or when some trifling and unimportant good qualities in me are rated at more than their proper value. But again I am in doubt: do I feel like this simply because I do not want a man who praises me to think about me differently from the way I think myself? And am I moved not so much by what is good for him as by the fact that those good qualities of mine which I approve of in myself are all the more pleasing to me when someone else approves of them too? For in a sense I am not being praised when my own opinion of myself is not praised, when, that is, qualities of mine are praised of which I myself do not approve, or when a high value is set on things in me which I regard as unimportant. It seems then that I am doubtful of myself in this matter.

Yes, Truth, in you I see that when I am praised the pleasure I feel should not be for my own sake but for the sake of the good of my neighbor. But whether this is really how I do feel I do not know. In this matter I know less of myself than of you. I beg you, my God, to show me myself, so that I may confess the fault that is in me to my brethren who will pray for me. Let me question myself again more carefully. If, when I hear myself praised, I am moved by thoughts of the good of my neighbor, why is it that I am less moved when someone else is unjustly blamed than when I myself am unjustly blamed? Why am I more wounded by a reproach leveled against me than by one which, with equal injustice, is, while I am present, leveled against someone else? Am I ignorant of this too? Or is not the fact simply this, that I deceive myself and in your presence fail to be truthful in heart and tongue? Put this madness far from me, Lord, lest my own mouth be to me the *sinner's oil to make fat my head.*

38

I AM POOR AND NEEDY, yet I am the better when, groaning secretly in my dissatisfaction with myself, I seek your mercy till the time comes when what is defective in me will be made good and brought to perfection in that peace which is unknown to the eye of the proud. Words which come from the mouth and actions which are known to men carry with them a most dangerous temptation from the love of praise which goes around as it were canvassing and collecting votes for the advancement of one's personal distinction. It still tempts me even when I condemn it in myself; indeed it tempts me even in the very act of condemning it; often in our contempt of vainglory we are merely being all the more vainglorious, and so one cannot really say that one glories in the contempt of glory; for one does not feel contempt for something in which one glories.

39

INSIDE US TOO is another evil belonging to the same class of temptation. It is the vanity of those who are pleased with themselves, however much they may not please others, or may displease them, or may not care whether they please them or not. But those who are pleased with themselves certainly do not please you. Here it is not so much a case of taking pleasure in things that are not good as though they were good; the fault is in taking pleasure in good things which come from you as though they came from oneself; or, even if they are acknowledged as coming from you, in assuming that one deserves to have them; or, even if it is admitted that they are due to your grace, in not rejoicing with their brethren but envying your grace to others. In all these and other similar dangers and difficulties you see the trembling of my heart, and often as you heal my wounds I feel new wounds being inflicted upon me.

40

WHEN HAVE YOU not walked with me, O Truth, teaching me what to beware of and what to seek after, when I referred to you what I have been able to see here below and asked your advice? With my outward senses I surveyed, to the best of my ability, the world, and I observed both the life which my body has from me and these senses themselves. From these I entered into the recesses of my memory, space folded upon huge space and all miraculously full of innumerable abundance, and I considered it and I was amazed; no one of all the things there could I discover without you, and I did not find any of them was you. Nor was I myself the discoverer, though I went through them all and tried to distinguish each from each, estimating them according to their proper worth, taking some things on the report of my senses, questioning others which I felt to be somehow parts of myself, and I counted and distinguished between these messengers, and now in the vast treasury of my memory I would meditate on something stored there, or put something away or take something out. But it was not I myself who did all this—that is to say, the power by which I did it was not myself—nor were you that power, because

you are the permanent and abiding light which I consulted on all these things, asking whether they are, what
they are, and what they are worth. And I heard you
teaching me and commanding me. And I often do this.
I find a delight in it, and whenever I can relax from my
necessary duties I have recourse to this pleasure. And in
all these things over which I range as I am consulting you
I find no secure place for my soul except in you, and in
you I pray that what is scattered in me may be brought
together so that nothing of me may depart from you. And
sometimes working within me you open for me a door
into a state of feeling which is quite unlike anything to
which I am used—a kind of sweet delight which, if I
could only remain permanently in that state, would be
something not of this world, not of this life. But my sad
weight makes me fall back again; I am swallowed up by
normality; I am held fast and heavily do I weep, but
heavily I am held. So much are we weighed down by the
burden of custom! Here I have the power but not the
wish to stay; there I wish to be but cannot; both ways,
miserable.

41

So, UNDER THE HEADINGS of the three forms of
concupiscence I have considered the sicknesses of my
sins, and I have called your right hand to my help.
For I have seen your splendor, but my own heart has
been wounded; I have been beaten back and have said:
Who can reach there? *I am cast away from the sight of
Thine eyes*. You are Truth presiding over everything.
But I in my covetousness, while not wanting to lose you,
wanted at the same time to possess a lie; just as no man

wants to speak so falsely that he himself ceases to be conscious of the truth. And this was why I lost you, because you will not be possessed together with a lie.

42

WHOM COULD I FIND to reconcile me to you? Was I to seek the help of angels? By what prayer, what sacraments? Many people in their attempts to return to you and not being able to do so by their own strength have, so I hear, tried this way and have fallen into a desire for strange visions and have become, rightly, the victims of delusions. For in seeking you they have drawn themselves up in the arrogance of their learning; they have thrown out their chests instead of beating their breasts, and so through likeness of heart they drew to themselves the *princes of the air* as their fellow-conspirators in pride and were deceived by them through magical powers. They were seeking a mediator through whom to become clean, but this was not he. It was the devil, *transforming himself into an angel of light,* and for proud flesh it proved a strong attraction that he himself had not a body of flesh. For they were mortal and sinners; you, Lord, to whom they wished to be reconciled, are immortal and without sin. So a mediator between God and men should have something in common with God and something in common with men. If he were in both respects like men, he would be far from God, and if he were in both respects like God, he would be far from men, and so neither way could he be a mediator. But that deceitful mediator, by whom, according to your secret judgment, pride deserves to be mocked, has one thing in common with men—namely, sin—and appears to have another thing in common with God—that is that, not being clothed in the mortality of flesh, he can pretend to be immortal. But, since *the wages of sin is death,* he has this in common with men—that he, like them, is condemned to death.

43

BUT THE TRUE mediator whom in your secret mercy you have shown to men and have sent Him so that they, by His example, might learn humility, that *Mediator between God and man, the Man Christ Jesus,* appeared between mortal sinners and the immortal Just One: mortal with men, just with God; so that, because the wages of justice is life and peace, He might, by a justice conjoined with God, make void the death of those sinners who were justified by Him; for He was willing to let that death be common both to Him and to them. He was revealed to the holy men of old so that they might be saved through faith in His passion that was to come, just as we may be saved through faith in His passion now that it is in the past. For insofar as He is man, He is mediator; but insofar as He is the Word, He is not midway between God and man; for He is equal to God, both God with God, and together one God.

How greatly have you loved us, good Father, who *sparedst not Thine only Son, but deliveredst Him up for us ungodly!* How you have loved us, for whom, *He that thought it no robbery to be equal with Thee, was made subject even to the death of the cross.* He alone *free among the dead, having power to lay down His life, and power to take it again:* for us He was to you both victor and victim, and victor because victim: for us He was to you both priest and sacrifice, and priest because sacrifice: and He made us sons to you instead of slaves by being born of you and by becoming your slave. With reason, then, my hope in Him is strong, that *Thou wilt heal all my infirmities* by Him who *sitteth at Thy right hand and maketh intercession for us;* otherwise I should despair. For many and great are my infirmities, many they are and great; but your medicine has more power still. We might have thought that your Word was far from any union with man, and we might have despaired, unless it had been *made flesh and dwelt among us.*

Terrified by my sins and the mass and weight of my misery, I had pondered in my heart a purpose of flight to the wilderness. But you forbade me and gave me strength by saying: *Therefore Christ died for all, that they which live may now no longer live unto themselves, but unto Him that died for them.* See, Lord, *I cast my care upon Thee,* that I may live and *consider wondrous things out of Thy law.* You know my unskillfulness and my weakness; teach me and heal me. He, your only Son, *in Whom are hid all the treasures of wisdom and knowledge,* has redeemed me with His blood. *Let not the proud speak evil of me,* for my thoughts are on the price of my redemption; I eat it and drink it and give it to others to eat and drink, and, being poor myself, I desire to be satisfied by it among those that *eat and are satisfied, and they shall praise the Lord who seek Him.*